From the Book of My Life

For David Trinidad,

NEW AND SELECTED POEMS

From The Book of My Life

by

Edward Field

Edward Field

The Sheep Meadow Press
Riverdale-on-Hudson, New York

Printed in the United States of America.

The Sheep Meadow Press, Riverdale-on-Hudson, N.Y.

Typesetting by Keystrokes, Lenox, Massachusetts

Distributed by Persea Books
225 Lafayette Street
New York, NY 10012

Library of Congress Catalog Card Number: 86-43208

ISBN 0-935296-68-9
ISBN 0-935296-69-7 (pbk.)

Contents

from STAND UP, FRIEND, WITH ME (1963)

Prologue

Look, friend, at this universe
With its spiral clusters of stars
Flying out all over space
Like bedsprings suddenly busting free;
And in this galaxy, the sun
Fissioning itself away,
Surrounded by planets, prominent in their dignity,
And bits and pieces running wild;
And this middling planet
With a lone moon circling round it.

Look, friend, through the fog of gases at this world
With its skin of earth and rock, water and ice,
With various creatures and rooted things;
And up from the bulging waistline
To this land of concrete towers,
Its roads swarming like a hive cut open,
Offshore to this island, long and fishshaped,
Its mouth to a metropolis,
And in its belly, this village,
A gathering of families at a crossways,
And in this house, upstairs and through the wide open door
Of the front bedroom with a window on the world,
Look, friend, at me.

Greece

This is a country where miracles occur:
The probability is in the air
That statues turn human if you kiss them;
And at any moment one expects a god
To step from the marble column, and indeed
They could not have remained standing for so long
If they were not still inhabited by gods.

Naturally one doesn't always expect to see
People wearing snakes for hair
Or satyrs chasing youths
Or charming gods turning into still more charming bulls,
But such things do occur.
One knows, for example, that men and goats
Copulate with fertile success.
Look now at this goat walking up the road
Led by a young Greek with a definite goatish look:
Goats and Greeks have lived together for so long
That there are many similarities,
Especially when they sing.

And of course if the Greek is not a shepherd
He is a seaman; for the sea is everywhere
And still sailed by sleek ships
And the monsters that habitually swallow them;
And everywhere are islands where sailors grow
Wise like olives to the lore of salt.

Though not quite as much admitted openly nowadays
The favorite occupation still is sex
And it is easy to know why
When you see their bodies as beautiful as ever,
With one exception, the Greeks that go to America.
Of course they come back to Greece if they can as we all do,
But they return with something gone out of them:

4

I suppose they sacrifice their gods to a foreign one
And lose their own divinity.

Hydra

This island whose name means water
Never had gods and temples as other Greek islands had;
It never was the home of monsters with ferocious heads
And maybe it wasn't even there.

But a few centuries ago
As though it had just risen from the sea
Men saw stones and pine trees on the slopes
And with the stones made houses and with the trees made ships.

And as naturally as fish swim
The ships went sailing;
And as naturally as the sun rises
The boys grew into heroes and sailed to war.

But the heroes were foolhardy as heroes are
So although they were brave and did amazing things
The ships were sunk at last
And the handsome heroes lay on the ocean floor.

Wars over, fame won, the island settled down,
But with the trees all gone the soil blew away to sea;
The houses began to crumble,
And the island bleached in the sun to anonymity.

The name means water but now even the wells are drying
And no one expects the rock to grow trees again;
While the waters push gently on its shores
Waiting for the island to sink quietly back into the sea.

Donkeys

They are not silent like workhorses
Who are happy or indifferent about the plow and wagon;
Donkeys don't submit like that
For they are sensitive
And cry continually under their burdens;
Yes, they are animals of sensibility
Even if they aren't intelligent enough
To count money or discuss religion.

Laugh if you will when they heehaw
But know that they are crying
When they make that noise that sounds like something
Between a squawking water pump and a foghorn.

And when I hear them sobbing
I suddenly notice their sweet eyes and ridiculous ears
And their naive bodies that look as though they never grew up
But stayed children, as in fact they are;
And being misunderstood as children are
They are forced to walk up mountains
With men and bundles on their backs.

Somehow I am glad that they do not submit without a protest
But as their masters are of the deafest
The wails are never heard.

I am sure that donkeys know what life should be
But, alas, they do not own their bodies;
And if they had their own way, I am sure
That they would sit in a field of flowers
Kissing each other, and maybe
They would even invite us to join them.

For they never let us forget that they know
(As everyone knows who stays as sweet as children)

That there is a far better way to spend time;
You can be sure of that when they stop in their tracks
And honk and honk and honk.

And if I tried to explain to them
Why work is not only necessary but good,
I am afraid that they would never understand
And kick me with their back legs
As commentary on my wisdom.

So they remain unhappy and sob
And their masters who are equally convinced of being right
Beat them and hear nothing.

Notes from a Slave Ship

It is necessary to wait until the boss's eyes are on you
Then simply put your work aside,
Slip a fresh piece of paper in the typewriter,
And start to write a poem.

Let their eyes boggle at your impudence;
The time for a poem is the moment of assertion,
The moment when you say I exist—
Nobody can buy my time absolutely.

Nobody can buy me even if I say, Yes I sell.
There I am sailing down the river,
Quite happy about the view of the passing towns,
When I find that I have jumped overboard.

There is always a long swim to freedom.
The worst of it is the terrible exhaustion
Alone in the water in the darkness,
The shore a fading memory and the direction lost.

A Bill to My Father

I am typing up bills for a firm to be sent to their clients.
It occurs to me that firms are sending bills to my father
Who has that way an identity I do not often realize.
He is a person who buys, owes, and pays,
Not papa like he is to me.
His creditors reproach him for not paying on time
With a bill marked "Please Remit."
I reproach him for never having shown his love for me
But only his disapproval.
He has a debt to me too
Although I have long since ceased asking him to come across;
He does not know how and so I do without it.
But in this impersonal world of business
He can be communicated with:
With absolute assurance of being paid
The boss writes "Send me my money"
And my father sends it.

The Statue of Liberty

All the ships are sailing away without me.
Day after day I hear their horns announcing
To the wage earners at their desks
That it is too late to get aboard.

They steam out of the harbor
With the statue of a French woman waving them good-by
Who used to be excellent to welcome people with
But is better lately for departures.

The French gave her to us as a reminder
Of their slogan and our creed
Which hasn't done much good
Because we have turned a perfectly good wilderness
Into a place nice to visit but not to live in.

Forever a prisoner in the harbor
On her star-shaped island of gray stones
She has turned moldy-looking and shapeless
And her bronze drapery stands oddly into the wind.

From this prison-like island
I watch the ships sailing away without me
Disappearing one by one, day after day,
Into the unamerican distance,

And in my belly is one sentence: *Set Freedom Free,*
As the years fasten me into place and attitude,
Hand upraised and face into the wind
That no longer brings tears to my eyes.

My Coldwater Flat

Now that it is winter my coldwater flat is cold:
The morning alarm wakes my seedy eyes to their first heroic
    look;
If they shut just once all is lost.
I light the oven that barely pushes out a bell of warmth,
Shave a ragged face that I do not dare study,
And brush the traces of digestion out of my mouth.
Saliva flows, my arms
Struggle with the clothes like with an enemy.
The toilet is far beyond this small place of comfort,
And it is only at the extremest necessity
That I dare to bare my behind:
Truly I am man braving the elements.

And only now, blinking behind my typewriter
In the dry warmth commerce provides its dependents
Can I appreciate the miracle that got me out of bed
And made me leave behind my strange and lovely dreams
For the world and its miseries, mankind and his hungers,
For a life of goose pimples and sweat
And the rare overwhelming flush of love.

The Dirty Floor

The floor is dirty:
Not only the soot from the city air
But a surprising amount of hair litters the room.
It is hard to keep up with. Even before
The room is all swept up it is dirty again.

We are shedding more than we realize.
The amount of hair I've shed so far
Could make sixty of those great rugs
The Duke of China killed his weavers for,
And strangle half the sons of Islam.

Time doesn't stop even while I scrub the floor
Though it seems that the mind empties like a bathtub,
That all the minds of the world go down the drain
Into the sewer; but hair keeps falling
And not for a moment can the floor be totally clean.

What is left of us after years of shitting and shedding?
Are we whom our mothers bore or some stranger now
With the name of son, but nameless,
Continually relearning the same words
That mean, with each retelling, less.

He whom you knew is a trail of leavings round the world.
Renewal is a lie: Who I was has no more kisses.
Barbara's fierce eyes were long ago swept up from her floor.
A stranger goes by the name of Marianne; it is not she,
Nor for that matter was the Marianne I knew.

The floor having accumulated particles of myself
I call it dirty; dirty, the streets thick with the dead;
Dirty, the thick air I am used to breathing.
I am alive at least. Quick, who said that?
Give me the broom. The leftovers sweep the leavings away.

Unwanted

The poster with my picture on it
Is hanging on the bulletin board in the Post Office.

I stand by it hoping to be recognized
Posing first full face and then profile

But everybody passes by and I have to admit
The photograph was taken some years ago.

I was unwanted then and I'm unwanted now
Ah guess ah'll go up echo mountain and crah.

I wish someone would find my fingerprints somewhere
Maybe on a corpse and say, You're it.

Description: Male, or reasonably so
Complexion white, but not lily-white

Thirty-fivish, and looks it lately
Five-feet-nine and one-hundred-thirty pounds: no physique

Black hair going gray, hairline receding fast
What used to be curly, now fuzzy

Brown eyes starey under beetling brow
Mole on chin, probably will become a wen

It is perfectly obvious that he was not popular at school
No good at baseball, and wet his bed.

His aliases tell his history: Dumbbell, Good-for-nothing,
Jewboy, Fieldinsky, Skinny, Fierce Face, Greaseball, Sissy.

Warning: This man is not dangerous, answers to any name
Responds to love, don't call him or he will come.

14

The Telephone

My happiness depends on an electric appliance
And I do not mind giving it so much credit
With life in this city being what it is
Each person separated from friends
By a tangle of subways and buses
Yes my telephone is my joy
It tells me that I am in the world and wanted
It rings and I am alerted to love or gossip
I go comb my hair which begins to sparkle
Without it I was like a bear in a cave
Drowsing through a shadowy winter
It rings and spring has come
I stretch and amble out into the sunshine
Hungry again as I pick up the receiver
For the human voice and the good news of friends

A Journey

When he got up that morning everything was different:
He enjoyed the bright spring day
But he did not realize it exactly, he just enjoyed it.

And walking down the street to the railroad station
Past magnolia trees with dying flowers like old socks
It was a long time since he had breathed so simply.

Tears filled his eyes and it felt good
But he held them back
Because men didn't walk around crying in that town.

And waiting on the platform at the station
The fear came over him of something terrible about to happen:
The train was late and he recited the alphabet to keep hold.

And in its time it came screeching in
And as it went on making its usual stops,
People coming and going, telephone poles passing,

He hid his head behind a newspaper
No longer able to hold back the sobs, and willed his eyes
To follow the rational weavings of the seat fabric.

He didn't do anything violent as he had imagined.
He cried for a long time, but when he finally quieted down
A place in him that had been closed like a fist was open,

And at the end of the ride he stood up and got off that train:
And through the streets and in all the places he lived in later on
He walked, himself at last, a man among men,
With such radiance that everyone looked up and wondered.

Sonny Hugg and the Porcupine

This baby porcupine squeezing into a crevice of rock
Could be hauled out into the open,
Poked with a stick, and otherwise toyed with,
But cute as he was he couldn't be kissed.

Love rose tender in the heart of Sonny Hugg
And he dreamed impossible dreams.
But all those bristles! His mind twisted and turned
To find a workable solution.

To hug this improbable child was important to him,
The child willing or no, and who could say it wasn't willing.
Maybe the Gillette, the garden shears ... No, without those spurs
This creature would be unlovable as a rat.

Sonny was versatile but this defeated him.
He faced reality. A porcupine for a lover?
Alas, he would have to settle for those creations
Not quite as darling but with bodies good for hugging.

Graffiti

Blessings on all the kids who improve the signs in the subways:
They put a beard on the fashionable lady selling soap,
Fix up her flat chest with the boobies of a chorus girl,
And though her hips be wrapped like a mummy
They draw a hairy cunt where she should have one.

The bathing beauty who looks pleased
With the enormous prick in her mouth, declares
"Eat hair pie; it's better than cornflakes."
And the little boy in the Tarzan suit eating white bread
Now has a fine pair of balls to crow about.

And as often as you wash the walls and put up your posters,
When you go back to the caged booth to deal out change
The bright-eyed kids will come with grubby hands.
Even if you watch, you cannot watch them all the time,
And while you are dreaming, if you have dreams anymore,

A boy and girl are giggling behind an iron pillar;
And although the train pulls in and takes them on their way
Into a winter that will freeze them forever,
They leave behind a wall scrawled all over with flowers
That shoot great drops of gism through the sky.

A New Cycle

My father buying me the bicycle that time
Was an unusual thing for him to do.
He believed that a parent's duty meant the necessities:
Food, clothing, shelter, and music lessons.

I had hardly dared to ask him for it
And I didn't believe he really meant to buy me one
Until I saw him take out the money and hand it over—
Eight dollars secondhand, but newly painted, and good rubber.

And I couldn't thank him, a hug was out of the question with us,
So I just got up on it and rode a ways shakily
And then I made him ride it—
He didn't even know he was supposed to say it was a good bike.

I rode off on it into a new life, paper route, pocket money,
Dances in other towns where the girls found me attractive,
And sexual adventures that would have made my father's hair
Stand up in horror had he known.

Daddy I can thank you now for the bike you gave me
Which meant more to me than you knew, or could have stood to know.
I rode away to everywhere it could take me, until finally
It took me to this nowhere, this noplace I am now.

I just passed my thirty-fifth birthday,
The end of a seven-year cycle and the beginning of a new one,
And sure enough I woke up the first day quite empty,
Everything over, with nothing to do and no ideas for the future.

Daddy whom I now can hug and kiss
Who gives me money when I ask,
What shall I do with this life you gave me
That cannot be junked like a bicycle when it wears out?

Is it utterly ridiculous for a man thirty-five years old and graying
To sit in his father's lap and ask for a bike? Even if he needs one?
Whom shall he ask if not his father?
Daddy, darling daddy, please buy me a bicycle.

Ode to Fidel Castro

I

O Boy God, Muse of Poets
Come sit on my shoulder while I write
Cuddle up and fill my poem with love
And even while I fly on billows of inspiration
Don't forget to tickle me now and then
For I am going to write on World Issues
Which demands laughter where we most believe.

Also, My Cute One, don't let me take a heroic pose
And act as though I know it all
Guard me from Poet's Head that dread disease
Where the words ring like gongs and meaning goes out the window
Remind me of the human size of truth
Whenever I spout a big, ripe absolute
(Oh why did you let the architects of our capital city
Design it for giants
So that a man just has to take a short walk and look about
For exhaustion to set in immediately)
Please, Sweet Seeker, don't discourage me from contradicting myself
But make everything sound like life, like people we like
And most of all give me strength not to lay aside this poem
Like so many others in the pile by my typewriter
But to write the whole thing from beginning to end
O Perfection, the way it wants to go.

II

My subject, Dear Muse, is Fidel Castro
Rebellissimo and darling of the Spanish-American lower classes
A general who adopted for his uniform
The work clothes of the buck private and the beard of the saints
A man fit for ruling a great nation
But who only has an island.

Irene, the beautiful Cuban, has his picture over her bed
Between Rudolph Valentino and the Blessed Virgin—
He stands large and flabby between the perfect body and the purest soul
Doves on his shoulders, on his open hands
And one dove for crown standing on his head—
He is not afraid of birdshit, his face is radiant.

Someday Hollywood will make a movie biography of his life
Starring the spreading Marlon Brando
They'll invent a great love on his way up, a blonde with a large crucifix
Whom he loses along with his idealism, and once at the top
A great passion, a dark whore with large breasts, to drag him down.
In real life his romance is with his people and his role
Otherwise his sex life is normal for his age and position.

Fidel, Fidel, Fidel...
I am in love with the spotlight myself
And would like the crowds to chant my name
Which has the same letters as yours but rearranged
Where is my island Where my people
What am I doing on this continent Where is my crown
Where did everyone go that used to call me king
And light up like votive candles when I smiled?
(I have given them all up for you sweet youth my muse
Be truly mine.)

Am I like Goethe who kept faith in Napoleon
Long after the rest of the world had given him up
For tyrant and betrayer of the revolution?
If Napoleon was like Tolstoy writing a novel
Organizing a vast army of plots and themes
Then Castro is like a poet writing an ode
(Alas that poets should be rulers—
Revise that line, cut that stanza, lop off that phrase)
Paredon! Paredon!

What he did was kick out the bad men and good riddance Batista
What he is doing... Well, what he is trying to do is...
(Muse, why don't you help me with this,
Are you scared of socialist experiment?)
One thing he is doing is upsetting a lot of people
Our papers are full of stories that make him out a devil
And you a fool if you like him
But they are against me too even if they don't know I exist
So let's shake Fidel
(The hand that exists shakes the hand that doesn't)
My Fidel Castro, Star of Cuba.

III

The Hotel Teresa in Harlem is a dumpy landmark in a slum
But when Fidel Castro went there to stay
And when Nikita Khrushchev went up and hugged and kissed
      him for being Mr. Wonderful
Right out in public (they get away with it those foreigners)
Then Harlem became the capital of the world
And the true home of the united nations.

That whole bunch sitting around the hotel like in bivouac roasting
      chickens
And all those Negroes looking at them bug-eyed—
Nobody that great ever came up there before to stay.
Of course plenty of people that great came out of Harlem
Like Jimmy Baldwin, not to mention those jazz people we all love
But the Colored that came out of Harlem like roman candles
You don't catch them going back there like a Fourth of July parade.
Now Cuba and Russia have gone to Harlem
And found it a good place for loving—
That Harlem, full of rats chewing off babies' arms
And social workers trying to keep the whole place from exploding
I used to have friends up there
When I went to visit them if I passed a mirror
My whiteness would surprise me

The mind takes on darkness of skin so easily
(Of course being a Jew I'm not exactly white)
It is that easy to turn black
And then have to be in that awful boat the Negroes are in
Although it's pretty lousy being white
And having that black hatred turned on you.

What after all can a white man say but, I'm ashamed
Hey fellas I'm sorry . . .
Unless you are President and then you have your golden opportunity.
Perhaps the only thing to do is look upon each other
As two men look when they meet solitary in the deep woods
Come black man let us jerk off together
Like boys do to get to know each other.

Well just like others who have escaped ghettos I don't go to
       Harlem anymore
I don't like to see the trapped whom I can't set free
But when I see the big front-page photos of Castro and
       Khrushchev hugging in Harlem
A widescreen spectacle with supermen in totalscope embrace, and
       in color yet
I sit back and dig it all the way.

IV

BOMBS GOING OFF ALL OVER HAVANA
In Rockefeller Center the Cuban Tourist Office is closed
And across the skating rink men are putting up
The world's largest Christmas tree which will never be Christian
Even if you cut it down, make it stand on cement, decorate it with balls
It will still scream for the forest, like a wild animal
Like the gods who love freedom and topple to the saws of commerce
The gods who frighten us half to death in our dreams with their doings
And disappear when we need them most, awake.

By the time you see this, Fidel, you might not even exist anymore
My government is merciless and even now

The machine to destroy you is moving into action
The chances are you won't last long
Well so long pal it was nice knowing you
I can't go around with a broken heart all my life
After I got over the fall of the Spanish Republic
I guess I can get over anything
My job is just to survive.
But I wish you well Fidel Castro
And if you do succeed in making that island
The tropic paradise God meant it to be
I'll be the first to cheer and come for a free visit if invited.

So you're not perfect, poets don't look for perfect
It's your spirit we love and the glamour of your style
I hope someday the cameras of the world
Are turned on you and me in some spot like Harlem
And then you'll get a kiss that will make Khrushchev's be forgotten
A kiss of the poet, that will make you truly good
The way you meant to be.

A Birthday Poem for My Little Sister

Ball of cold metals, shooter of nerve rays, Moon,
Be god yet for poets and their strange loves
Call in the tides of madness that trip us on our way
And help me send a poem of love to my sweet sister
Still darling like when she was a baby
Although now woman-shaped and married.

Dear Barbara, when you had the ear operation
And your hair was cut short like a baby dike
I sat by your crib because I considered you mine
And read you stories of cluck-cluck and moo-moo:
They didn't have to make sense, just noises.

I tried to keep you from masturbating
According to instructions in Parents' Magazine
Which recommended the diversion method rather than threats or
        punishment.
It was no use, your hand preferred your little cunt to toys I offered
Like the ape in the zoo who was jerking off
And all the kids asked their mothers, "What's he doing, ma?"
So the keeper tried to divert him from his hard-on with an ice-cream cone
But he shifted the cone to the other hand and licked it while he
        went right on.

And then during the war we were both in uniform
You in the Brownies and I in the Air Force:
When I came home that time with silver wings on
You threw yourself into my arms like a furry bundle;
That was your contribution to the war effort, a hug for a soldier
Not bombing the Germans as you were convinced the Brownies
        were going to do.
When you were twelve I saw your intellectual possibilities
And took you to a difficult play
Where you fell in love with a faggot actor.
Then I tried modern poetry on you, The Love Song of J. Alfred Prufrock;

You listened very seriously and remembered the refrain like a
    jump-rope poem:
It was odd to hear a little girl reciting those lines.

And suddenly you grew up and went out with boys...strangers
And you spoke with them in a language like a code
I mean you became a woman, so I'll never have you again:
There must be a taboo against brothers.
Of course now I have someone of my own who reaches to me
    with sweet arms
But the heart is a tree of many seasons
And old loves grow forever deep inside.

The moon rules old loves in their branching
And today the great white magic ball in the sky
Has wound up my heart like on a line of wool
Today on your birthday I remember
How I ran up and down the block knocking on all the doors
To tell the neighbors you were born
(Bored looks, after all you were the sixth child):
I was really announcing that you were born for me and would be mine.

But you grew up and went away and got married
As little girls grow up into women
Leaving us gasping and desperate and hurt.
And we recover and forget, or half-forget
Until sitting down to write a birthday poem we remember everything—
A little girl on her potty hunched seriously to the business
Or holding all of you at once in my arms, colt, calf, and pussy-cat:
All I mean is, I miss you my little sister.

Mark Twain and Sholem Aleichem

Mark Twain and Sholem Aleichem went one day to Coney Island—
Mark wearing a prison-striped bathing costume and straw hat,
Sholem in greenish-black suit, starched collar, beard,
Steel-rimmed schoolmaster glasses, the whole works,
And an umbrella that he flourished like an actor
Using it sometimes to hurry along the cows
As he described scenes of childhood in the village in Poland,
Or to spear a Jew on a sword like a cossack.

Sitting together on the sand among food wrappers and lost coins,
They went through that famous dialogue
Like the vaudeville routine, After-you-Gaston:
"They tell me you are called the Yiddish Mark Twain."
"Nu? The way I heard it you are the American Sholem Aleichem."
And in this way passed a pleasant day admiring each other,
the voice of the old world and the voice of the new.

"Shall we risk the parachute jump, Sholem?"
"Well, Markele, am I properly dressed for it?
Better we should go in the water a little maybe?"
So Sholem Aleichem took off shoes and socks (with holes—a shame),
Rolled up stiff-serge pants showing his varicose veins;
And Mark Twain, his bathing suit moth-eaten and gaping
In important places, lit up a big cigar,
And put on a pair of waterwings like an angel.

The two great writers went down where the poor
Were playing at the water's edge
Like a sewer full of garbage, warm as piss.
Around them shapeless mothers and brutal fathers
Were giving yellow, brown, white, and black children
Lessons in life that the ignorant are specially qualified to give:
Slaps and scoldings, mixed with food and kisses.

Mark Twain, impetuous goy, dived right in,
And who could resist splashing a little the good-natured Jew?
Pretty soon they were both floundering in the sea
The serge suit ruined that a loving daughter darned and pressed,
The straw hat floating off on the proletarian waters.

They had both spent their lives trying to make the world a better place
And both had gently faced their failure.
If humor and love had failed, what next?
They were both drowning and enjoying it now,
Two old men of the two worlds, the old and the new,
Splashing about in the sea like crazy monks.

Tulips and Addresses

The Museum of Modern Art on West Fifty-third Street
Is interested only in the flower not the bulb:
After the Dutch tulips finished blooming in the garden last year
They pulled them up and threw them away—that place has no heart.
Some fortunately were rescued and came into my possession.

I kept them all winter in a paper bag from the A & P
At first where I was living then on the West Side
Until the next-door tribe of Murphies drove me out with rock and roll,
Then at Thompson Street in the Village where overhead
A girl and her lover tromped around all night on each other.

And that wasn't the end of it: I shlepped those bulbs around
For two months from place to place looking for a home,
All that winter, moving . . . Oy—although this was nothing new for me
Coming as I do from a wandering race,
And life with its ten plagues making me even more Jewish.

Now I am living on Abingdon Square, not the Ritz exactly, but a place
And I have planted the tulips in my window box:
Please God make them come up, so that everyone who passes by
Will know I'm there, at least long enough to catch my breath,
When they see the bright red beautiful flowers in my window.

The Sleeper

When I was the sissy of the block who nobody wanted on their team
Sonny Hugg persisted in believing that my small size was an asset
Not the liability and curse I felt it was
And he saw a use for my swift feet with which I ran away from fights.

He kept putting me into complicated football plays
Which would have been spectacular if they worked:
For instance, me getting clear in front and him shooting the ball over—
Or the sensation of the block, the Sleeper Play
In which I would lie down on the sidelines near the goal
As though resting and out of action, until the scrimmage began
And I would step onto the field, receive the long throw
And to the astonishment of all the tough guys in the world
Step over the goal line for a touchdown.

That was the theory anyway. In practice
I had the fatal flaw of not being able to catch
And usually had my fingers bent back and the breath knocked out of me
So the plays always failed, but Sonny kept on trying
Until he grew up out of my world into the glamorous
Varsity crowd, the popular kids of Lynbrook High.

But I will always have this to thank him for:
That when I look back on childhood
(That four psychiatrists haven't been able to help me bear the thought of)
There is not much to be glad for
Besides his foolish and delicious faith
That, with all my oddities, there was a place in the world for me
If only he could find the special role.

At the Coney Island Aquarium: An Ode for Ookie, the Older Walrus Child or The Sibling Rival

Do not worry, sweet little walrus, about the superior cuteness
Of those two new babies they brought to share your pool.

You keep pushing the twins out of the way
More concerned about keeping them from getting attention
Than having your own scrub-brush nose whiskers rubbed
So that no one gets the chance to give you
The endless hugs and kisses you deserve.

It is impossible of course to be more popular than twins
So finally you sink to the bottom and play dead
Hoping our hearts break—mine does anyway
And the Keeper watches anxiously, so you see it works.
But how long can you sit at the bottom of the water
When lungs cry for air and the heart for love?

No, Ookie, don't seek indiscriminate love from the many
As those two simple-minded children do
Who have not yet met with heartbreak (although they will),
But leap the railing right into my arms
And squirm there fishily always, Ookie, mine alone.

The Garden

The plants on the window ledges are all growing well
Except the avocado which is dying

The grapefruit seeds from breakfast came up
And the watermelon are sprouting all over the window box

The mango practically exploded it looked so pregnant
Cherry, peach, apple and plum trees flourish

The potato eyes threw up weird white shoots
And the birdseed grew a good crop of ragweed

We have formed a colony in a strange land
Planting our seeds and making ourselves at home

I look around, everything in order
The implements of living stacked

Fishes in the stream blowing bubbles like kisses
Wild cats to drag yowling from the woods

Trees to hug and roots to dig
A young horse to play around with

It is a beautiful place to have the run of
When a sweet creature of your own brings all of it to you.

from ESKIMO SONGS AND STORIES (1973)

The Giant Bear

There once was a giant bear
who followed people for his prey.
He was so big he swallowed them whole:
Then they smothered to death inside him
if they hadn't already died of fright.

Either the bear attacked them on the run,
or if they crawled into a cave
where he could not squeeze his body in,
he stabbed them with his whiskers like toothpicks,
drawing them out one by one,
and gulped them down.

No one knew what to do
until a wise man went out and let the bear swallow him,
sliding right down his throat into the dark, hot, slimy stomach.
And once inside, took his knife
and simply cut him open,
killing him of course.

He carved a door in the bear's belly
and threw out those who had been eaten before,
and then out he stepped himself
and went home to get help with the butchering.

Everyone lived on bear meat for a long time.
That's the way it goes:
Monster one minute, food the next.

An Eskimo Taunts His Rival
in Singing and Hunting

I know you, my friend. The way you talk
one would think you never lost a race.
Well, I dare you: The next time
a caribou with a rack of great antlers
swims across that lake over there
and the weather is so cold the kayaks ice up
making them really hard to paddle,
let's chase it then,
I mean let's just the two of us race
with our wives watching from the shore:
Remember that time
long ago when the two of us were young
and the kayaks went like a pack of wolves
after a caribou out on the big lake there?
I clearly remember you couldn't paddle nearly fast enough
but trailed well behind—
behind ME, my friend.
And you expect me to sing your praises now?

Grandma Takes a Foster Child

Grandma turned a little odd in spring:
She took a caterpillar in and mothered it.
She put it down her sleeve
while she went about her work,
letting it suck like a baby on her skin,
and soon it grew so big and fat and happy
it said, Jeetsee-jeetsee.

Her grandchildren saw this and were disgusted—
after all, a caterpillar!
So when grandma went behind the tent to pee,
they threw it to the sled-dogs
who gobbled the juicy tidbit up.

And when grandma came back in
she called, My darling? My own one?
Why don't I hear the song that made my old heart young again?
Where is my dear one that went Jeetsee?
Gone?
And she sat down crying by the fire alone.

The Woman Who Turned to Stone

A woman once refused to get married
and turned down every man who proposed to her,
so finally one of them said:
"You've got a heart of stone
I hope you turn into stone!"
And before she could answer with her famous sharp tongue
his words began to come true
and she could no longer move
from the spot where she was standing by the lake.
She was really turning into stone from the legs up.
Desperately she called to some kayaks paddling by:
"Kayaks, please come here boys,
I'm ready to get married now."
(Now she was willing to marry not just one
but as many as she could get!)
But the men wouldn't come near her
having been rejected too often.
She clapped her hands and sang her song:
"Kayaks everywhere,
please come here,
I'll take you all as husbands now.
Men, have pity on me
before my precious hands
have turned to stone."
But then her hands turned to stone,
stone was her tongue,
and her song was done.

Courting Song

The Owl saw the Plover crying and asked,
"Why are you crying, my pretty bird?"

"My husband, my poor husband," the Plover sobbed.
"A man caught him in a snare, and I have lost him."

"Well," said the Owl, "then why don't you take me,
handsome me, for your next husband,
with my bushy eyebrows and long beard,
my plump feathers and lofty forehead?"

"Huh," said the Plover, "who would have you, I wonder,
even with your plump feathers and long beard,
your lofty forehead and bushy eyebrows?
Look at you, you have no neck and stubby legs!"

The Owl hollered back, "You dirty bird,
so you won't have me for a husband?
Then I hope you end up a tidbit between someone's teeth!"

Lazy Eskimo

When I go out for caribou cow
I get myself a caribou cow.
But my friend, some hunter he is:
he's lazy as a dog. Big shot,
he's lying in the igloo dreaming of big game.

Friend, you'd better practice on caribou
before you go out on the ice
and face the claws and jaws of the white bear
or the horns of the musk ox charging you,
poor you and your little spear.

Beauty Cure (from Variety Photoplays)

When I was just a girl
I once took a beauty treatment
recommended by our medicine man:
Grandma took me out
and found old dried-up dog turds for me.
I had to put each turd on my tongue
keeping it in my mouth until it was soft,
then rub myself with it
all over my breasts and stomach.
That is where I got my lovely figure and vitality from.
For as the medicine man said,
dogshit used in the right way
possesses magic powers
and is a kind of elixir of youth.
That is why I still look so young
in spite of my great age.
So for a beautiful complexion, ladies,
I do not hesitate to recommend dogshit lotion to you.
Try some today!

from VARIETY PHOTOPLAYS (1967)

Curse of the Cat Woman

It sometimes happens
that the woman you meet and fall in love with
is of that strange Transylvanian people
with an affinity for cats.

You take her to a restaurant, say, or a show,
on an ordinary date, being attracted
by the glitter in her slitty eyes and her catlike walk,
and afterwards of course you take her in your arms
and she turns into a black panther
and bites you to death.

Or perhaps you are saved in the nick of time
and she is tormented by the knowledge of her tendency:
That she daren't hug a man
unless she wants to risk clawing him up.

This puts you both in a difficult position—
panting lovers who are prevented from touching
not by bars but by circumstance:
You have terrible fights and say cruel things
for having the hots does not give you a sweet temper.

One night you are walking down a dark street
and hear the pad-pad of a panther following you,
but when you turn around there are only shadows,
or perhaps one shadow too many.

You approach, calling, "Who's there?"
and it leaps on you.
Luckily you have brought along your sword
and you stab it to death.

And before your eyes it turns into the woman you love,
her breast impaled on your sword,

her mouth dribbling blood saying she loved you
but couldn't help her tendency.

So death released her from the curse at last,
and you knew from the angelic smile on her dead face
that in spite of a life the devil owned,
love had won, and heaven pardoned her.

Frankenstein

The monster has escaped from the dungeon
where he was kept by the Baron,
who made him with knobs sticking out from each side of his neck
where the head was attached to the body
and stitching all over
where parts of cadavers were sewed together.

He is pursued by the ignorant villagers,
who think he is evil and dangerous because he is ugly
and makes ugly noises.
They wave firebrands at him and cudgels and rakes,
but he escapes and comes to the thatched cottage
of an old blind man playing on the violin Mendelssohn's "Spring Song."

Hearing him approach, the blind man welcomes him:
"Come in, my friend," and takes him by the arm.
"You must be weary," and sits him down inside the house.
For the blind man has long dreamed of having a friend
to share his lonely life.

The monster has never known kindness—the Baron was cruel—
but somehow he is able to accept it now,
and he really has no instincts to harm the old man,
for in spite of his awful looks he has a tender heart:
Who knows what cadaver that part of him came from?

The old man seats him at table, offers him bread,
and says, "Eat, my friend." The monster
rears back roaring in terror.
"No, my friend, it is good. Eat—gooood"
and the old man shows him how to eat,
and reassured, the monster eats
and says, "Eat—gooood,"
trying out the words and finding them good too.

The old man offers him a glass of wine,
"Drink, my friend. Drink—gooood."
The monster drinks, slurping horribly, and says,
"Drink—gooood," in his deep nutty voice
and smiles maybe for the first time in his life.

Then the blind man puts a cigar in the monster's mouth
and lights a large wooden match that flares up in his face.
The monster, remembering the torches of the villagers,
recoils, grunting in terror.
"No, my friend, smoke—gooood,"
and the old man demonstrates with his own cigar.
The monster takes a tentative puff
and smiles hugely, saying, "Smoke—gooood,"
and sits back like a banker, grunting and puffing.

Now the old man plays Mendelssohn's "Spring Song" on the violin
while tears come into our dear monster's eyes
as he thinks of the stones of the mob, the pleasures of mealtime,
the magic new words he has learned
and above all of the friend he has found.

It is just as well that he is unaware—
being simple enough to believe only in the present—
that the mob will find him and pursue him
for the rest of his short unnatural life,
until trapped at the whirlpool's edge
he plunges to his death.

The Bride of Frankenstein

The Baron has decided to mate the monster,
to breed him perhaps,
in the interests of pure science, his only god.

So he goes up into his laboratory
which he has built in the tower of the castle
to be as near the interplanetary forces as possible,
and puts together the prettiest monster-woman you ever saw
with a body like a pin-up girl
and hardly any stitching at all
where he sewed on the head of a raped and murdered beauty queen.

He sets his liquids burping, and coils blinking and buzzing,
and waits for an electric storm to send through the equipment
the spark vital for life.
The storm breaks over the castle
and the equipment really goes crazy
like a kitchen full of modern appliances
as the lightning juice starts oozing right into that pretty corpse.

He goes to get the monster
so he will be right there when she opens her eyes,
for she might fall in love with the first thing she sees as ducklings do.
That monster is already straining at his chains and slurping,
ready to go right to it:
He has been well prepared for coupling
by his pinching leering keeper who's been saying for weeks,
"Ya gonna get a little nookie, kid,"
or "How do you go for some poontang, baby?"
All the evil in him is focused on this one thing now
as he is led into her very presence.

She awakens slowly,
she bats her eyes,
she gets up out of the equipment,

and finally she stands in all her seamed glory,
a monster princess with a hairdo like a fright wig,
lightning flashing in the background
like a halo and a wedding veil,
like a photographer snapping pictures of great moments.

She stands and stares with her electric eyes,
beginning to understand that in this life too
she was just another body to be raped.
The monster is ready to go:
He roars with joy at the sight of her,
so they let him loose and he goes right for those knockers.
And she starts screaming to break your heart
and you realize that she was just born:
In spite of her big tits she was just a baby.

But her instincts are right—
rather death than that green slobber:
She jumps off the parapet.
And then the monster's sex drive goes wild.
Thwarted, it turns to violence, demonstrating sublimation crudely;
and he wrecks the lab, those burping acids and buzzing coils,
overturning the control panel so the equipment goes off like a bomb,
the stone castle crumbling and crashing in the storm,
destroying them all . . . perhaps.

Perhaps somehow the Baron got out of that wreckage of his dreams
with his evil intact, if not his good looks,
and more wicked than ever went on with his thrilling career.
And perhaps even the monster lived
to roam the earth, his desire still ungratified;
and lovers out walking in shadowy and deserted places
will see his shape loom up over them, their doom—
and children sleeping in their beds
will wake up in the dark night screaming
as his hideous body grabs them.

The Life of Joan Crawford

For Barbara Barry

She was a working girl from a small town
but the town wasn't so small
that it didn't have a railroad track
dividing the right side from the wrong side.
On the right side was the Hill
where the swells lived in big houses,
and on the wrong side, the Hollow where the proletariat
spent their greasy and unrewarding lives.
(For in those days the American town
was a living demonstration of Marxist theory.)

Joan of course lived in the Hollow
in one of those shacks with sagging porches
the mill put up rows of for the workers.
Her father, Tim Crawford, was the town drunk
living on relief and odd jobs
ever since the mines closed down when Joan was a baby.
He had been waiting for them to reopen for twenty years.
Joan never knew what had happened to her mother:
Joan's birth, her mother's disappearance or death, the mine's closing,
that was in a time of violence no one would discuss.
Just mention it and her father went on a binge,
not that he was ever sober.

She sighed, and went off to work in the five-and-ten
wearing her made-over dress with little washable collar and cuffs.
Even with her prole accent and the cheap bag and shoes
she was a good looker.
Men used to come by in their flashy suits and big cigars,
call her tootsie and ask for a date,
but she knew a poor girl didn't stand a chance with them.
She wasn't one of those innocents
who think a guy loves you if he gets a hard-on.
Yet she wouldn't go with any of the boys from the Hollow either

51

because with them the future was sleazy with kids
and the ruin of her figure before she was thirty—
and no fun after the honeymoon
except the Friday-night fight
when he would come home stinking, having drunk up the paycheck
and beat her black and blue
when she threw the stack of overdue bills at him—
and then screw her viciously on the dining-room table.
Some fun.
That was life in the Hollow and she wasn't having any.
She had turned down a job working in the mill
where the pay was better but life closed like a trap on you
and chose the more ladylike job at the five-and-ten
where people called her Miss and she could pose genteelly
behind the Tangee cosmetic display and the ribbon counter.
For Joan had the makings of a lady
if she could ever get some dough to fix herself up with
and a speech teacher to correct her dreadful accent.

But Nature had its way with Joan at last:
Spring came and handsome John Wainrich
(of the best family in town—they owned everything,
the five-and-dime, the shut mines, and the mill),
John Wainrich came in one day to collect the receipts or something
and found a million-dollar baby in his own five-and-ten-cents store.
Well Joan fell hard
and went out with him in his big car
and of course in the moonlight she let him have his way with her.
She used to meet him on the sly
when he could get away from the country club
and the milk-white debutante he was engaged to,
and they would drive out to roadhouses
where he wouldn't be seen by his swell friends.
Joan had pride,
but what is a woman's pride when she's in love.
What it came to, a few months later,
was that she got pregnant,

and just as she was about to break the good news,
he told her he was going to be married
and would have to stop seeing her until after the wedding,
that it was just a marriage of convenience
and wouldn't make any difference to them.
So she couldn't tell him then, she would have died first.
My great love, she muttered sarcastically,
he didn't even use a scum-bag.
And she went off to the city
where she got a job as receptionist in an office.
Her boss, Mr. Harris, was an older but dignified man
with a wife at home on Park Avenue, the victim of neurosis and wealth—
with all that money she could buy neither health nor happiness.
Joan used to listen to Mr. Harris's troubles
when she brought him his alka-seltzer mornings.
And when she was promoted to secretary, they would have dinner out
and she'd advise him on business,
she being a girl with a good head on her shoulders.

In Mr. Harris's company she saw the world and learned fast.
She lost her small-town look and learned to dress,
wearing hat and gloves, to fluff out her hair
and drink vermouth cocktails.
And while retaining the colorful idiom of the Hollow,
her grammar improved and her voice lost its nasal whine.
Joan was a knockout in every way
from honest eyes and square shoulders
to the narrow hips of a tango dancer.

Nothing showed yet in the baby department.
At night Joan looked critically at herself in the mirror:
Not a bulge, but baby was in there all right,
and her eyes went bitter as she thought of its father—
her great love, hmph.
"Well young feller, at least we'll have each other.
But I'd better be making preparations.
A working girl can't leave things to the caterer."

Then her boss proposed: He'd divorce his wife and marry her.
"Gee Mr. Harris, I think you're swell but I can't.
There is a real big favor you could do for me, though,"
and she told him how she gave her all for love
and her lover turned out to be a louse.
So Mr. Harris set her up in a little flat until the baby came.
He didn't make any demands on her or anything,
not yet anyway: It was sort of a promissory note
to be paid off later when she grew to love him out of gratitude.

But her ex-lover, John Wainrich, came to town
with his new wedding ring on, and tracked her down;
and misunderstanding the arrangement, called her a few names,
but swore she was his and he'd never give her up.
Joan still loved him but had the courage
to flee to a cheap hotel.
She got a job as dance-hall hostess, dime-a-dance,
six months pregnant, but with a brave smile
as the customers stepped on her toes.
They found her a good joe and a willing ear
as they told her their troubles
while rubbing off against her to a slow foxtrot.
One of her customers, impressed by her dancing,
got her to enter a dance marathon with him for prize money—
she needed that dough for the little stranger—
but the strain was too much for her,
marathon-dancing in her seventh month!

She came to on a hospital bed
with no makeup on and a white cloth over her forehead like a nun
to see her griddle-faced father looking down on her,
his mouth boozy as ever, but in his heart
vowing to go on the wagon if God would spare her life:
"Come home with me, Joanie, I'll take care of you."
"And baby too, papa?"
"Didn't they tell you, Joanie? The baby..."
"Oh no..."

And tears of mourning still in her eyes
she went back to the Hollow and kept house for her father.

She had two visits shortly after returning home:
First, John's pale bride came by, big with child,
neglect driving her to seek out her rival.
When she saw Joan so sweet and good
instead of some tramp homewrecker type,
she burst into tears and confessed she knew John didn't love her
but hoped he would when the baby was born, his heir.
The bitterness in Joan's heart turned to pity—
weren't they both women who had suffered?—
so she forgave her and they wept together:
Joan never could resist being a pal.

The other visit was from old Mr. Wainrich, John's father.
(Never had the Hollow seen so many long cars drive through.)
The old capitalist had a confession to make:
"When I saw you at the window watering the geraniums
I could have sworn you were your mother."
"You knew my mother, Mr. Wainrich?" asked Joan astonished.
"Yes. Bette wasn't like the other women in the Hollow.
She was a Davis you know. Her parents
had been plantation people down in Georgia
and even if they did end up here in the Hollow
she never forgot that she was a thoroughbred."
"Are you trying to tell me that you loved my mother?" Joan gasped.

"Yes, I loved her, but the heir to an industrial empire
isn't free to marry whom he chooses,
so my family chose an appropriate bride for me.
At that time I was running our coal mines here,
where Tim Crawford worked.
He was the biggest and toughest man in the Hollow
so naturally he was spokesman for the boys.
He had loved your mother for years
but she knew what it meant for a woman to marry a miner

and live in constant fear of a cave-in.
And she hated his coarse language and crude manners: she was a lady.
And besides, she loved me.
But when I broke the news of my engagement to her
(I explained it was just a marriage of convenience
and it wouldn't make any difference to us)
she married Tim just to spite me.
But it wasn't enough for her: right on my wedding day
she got Tim Crawford to call the men out on strike,
and, with violence surging around the Hill,
I had the biggest wedding ever seen in these parts.
I was coal and my bride was steel: what a merger!
The President came, and there were reporters from Chicago,
and your mother, already big with child, leading a picket line.

That strike went on for months, and you were born in the middle of it.
But we couldn't go on apart, your mother and I.
We knew we were sinners, but we managed to meet on the sly,
although the strike had turned the town into a battlefield
and we belonged to opposing armies.
Finally we decided to run away together, but just at that time
a load of scabs I was importing to work the mines arrived,
and there was a tremendous battle between them and the miners,
led by Tim Crawford of course.
The miners had lead pipes and dynamite,
but we had the National Guard in full battle dress.
Your mother and I, eloping, got caught in the middle
and took refuge in a deserted mine;
and I don't know which side did it, but a stick of dynamite
was thrown down the shaft, and your mother
was buried by a ton of falling rock."
(Joan moaned and hid her face in her hands.)
"It was useless to do anything so I left her there.
Why say anything when no one knew?
She was destroyed by the strike she had started.
The mines were shut down for good of course,
I couldn't bear the memory.

They would have had to be shut anyway,
we were losing money on them."
"And that's why daddy never knew what happened to mother,
raising me all by himself, and took to drink..."
"Yes, and I went back home to my wife and our little John was born
and I tried to forget..."
"Promise me one thing, Mr. Wainrich," Joan said,
"for the sake of my mother's memory,
that you'll open the mines again and give daddy back his old job."

Joan had a lot to think about in the days that followed.
One day she got a call to come up right away to the big house,
and arriving, found John's wife dying,
having given birth to a child, and asking for her.
The pale bride lay holding her child, the Wainrich heir,
but seeing Joan, she sat up with her last strength and said,
"I give him to you," and fell back dead.
Joan fainted away, and when she came to,
it seemed a long time later, after the funeral and the mourning,
John Wainrich held her in his arms and was saying over and over,
"I am yours now, she gave me to you."
"But she meant the child," Joan cried.
"Both of us are yours, my darling."

So Joan found her place in life at last.
They always said she'd make it up there, surrounded by the help,
a lady, moving gracefully among the guests.
And what a difference now:
The miners in tuxes standing around the punchbowl with the swells,
the colored butler joining in the fun with loud yaks,
a new era, the classless society,
brought about by the smartest little woman in the U.S.A.,
Ladies and Gentlemen: Miss Joan Crawford.

Nancy

When scolded by Aunt Fritzy Ritz
Nancy seems to lose her wits.
Nancy is very often cross
but Fritzy's the undisputed boss.
She sits in the house reading the papers
supervising Nancy's capers.

Aunt Fritzy's a peculiar sort:
She has no visible means of support.
She never seems to earn a bean
and there's no "uncle" on the scene.
The questions seem to rise a lot:
Is Fritzy Nancy's aunt, or not?
If Fritzy is related to
that awful Mrs. Meany who
Annie Roonie had to flee,
then who can Nancy really be?

Rumors are flying thick and fast;
stories from mouth to ear are passed:
"Who is Fritzy Ritz indeed
but someone overcome by greed.
Welfare pays a monthly sum
to keep that orphan in her home.
Although she looks like Etta Kett
she's older, more depraved, in debt."

One scandalous version I have heard
(of which I don't believe a word)
says Nancy's father, coming back
a little early from the track,
found his wife and Fritzy in
a most revolting act of sin.
With a knife he tried to nip
this lesbian relationship:

Saw red, and stabbed; the blow went wild
and made an orphan of his child.
His wife was dead, he got the chair,
the court named Fritzy Ritz as heir.
The child, the house, the bank account,
were left to Fritzy Ritz, the "aunt."

No one will make Aunt Fritzy crawl
now that she's in charge of all:
the house, the grounds, the little brat.
She'll teach her to remember that!

Poor Nancy's nature has been bent
by this negative environment.
She never will grow up at all
but stay forever three feet tall.

Book of the Dead

An island in the fog. Waves lapping.
Strange movements. Figures digging graves.
Our boat approaches silently.
We have come to rescue Divina
from the mad doctor
who uses the blood of virgins
for a serum to restore his wife's beauty,
poor Madame Imperia who always wears a mask
imploring him to work harder, cursing her fate.

He has an army of half-human slaves,
their brains replaced by those of dogs,
and a chief assistant Igor,
whose mother was a Siberian witch
and his father a British scientist on an expedition
to locate frozen mammoths
for a meat-packing concern.
Igor rules the army of dogmen
with a whip and a sharp boot in the butt.

Now as we come nearer there is the sound
of barking voices, shovels on stone,
and an occasional yelping
as Igor kicks a lazy cur in the ribs
or the whip separates snarling mad dogmen
going for each others' throats.

Are we too late?
Have they already drained Divina's blood
for the vain Madame Imperia
to make her young again?
The boat slips into the cove,
we gather up the equipment for the rescue
and steal into the woods around the house
of mad doctor Cranshaw,

a benevolent-looking dwarf from Groton, Massachusetts,
who fell into the clutches of Madame Imperia.
She had chosen him
because of his high marks in chemistry at M.I.T.
and his personal fortune
for she knew that getting back your looks costs plenty.
They were married at a society wedding in Newport
after which she took off her undetectable plastic face
and showed him her true one, so horrible
that he bought the island and set up a laboratory there
to search for a lotion
that would restore her beauty.

Now for twenty years girls had been disappearing
until most recently our heroine Divina
was snatched from her prayers
at the grotto of Our Lady of Loreto.
At first everyone supposed she had run off to be a hippy.
That's where girls used to go,
into the international druggy scene
until they turned up in a basement dead
from the O.D.'s with tracks up and down their arms,
or sometimes with two little teeth marks at the throat
and strangely drained of blood.
Divina had dropped acid a few times
but she was no junkie,
and she was into the I Ching and the Jesus prayer
but she was no hippy.
Anyway, nobody is a hippy anymore.
Nowadays girls go into the feminist movement,
and if they disappear, it's into the radical lesbian underground
holding up banks and blowing up bridges.
Well, Divina had swung a little both ways—
we both led a hip life-style—
but she was no dyke, I'll swear to that.
She was really crazy about me, if you know what I mean—
she was my chick, she was in trouble,

so the Chief assigned me to the case:
It was ready Eddie to the rescue!

Now we were approaching the house through the dark trees,
brushing away cobwebs from our faces, ugh.
In a clearing ahead two dogmen carried something
horrible and writhing off into the bushes.
Inside the house through the lighted window
the doctor was experimenting on one of the dogmen.
Everybody was busy at his tasks
except Madame Imperia
who only sat around veiled and cursing,
ordering the dogmen to bring her this and that,
polishing her nails, and filing them razor sharp.

Forward. We plant a stick
of nerve gas by the window
and set it off with a glass-shattering boom.
All inhabitants are paralyzed for fifteen minutes.
We race through the house calling Divina. Divina.
No Divina.
The mad dwarf doctor's eyes are bulging
and Madame Imperia's are glittering,
and Igor has murder in his—
for the gas does not put you out
and your brain goes right on figuring
and they were all thinking what to do about us
when the gas wore off:
They had a few tricks up their sleeves all right.

Minutes were ticking by. Ah, cages.
But we don't dare let loose the sub-human monsters there,
all operated on unsuccessfully by the mad Cranshaw.
Now a door to the basement, but sealed.
Search for a button in the wall.
No, not a button, an electric eye.
Break the beam and the door slides open.

62

Steps going down, an underground lab
with who? Yes, Divina
strapped to a table
breasts bulging up from thongs cutting into her flesh,
thighs writhing to protect her tender loins.
From the look of things
those dogmen had been having quite a go at her,
but apart from slaver on her face
and puddles of green dog come on her belly
it doesn't look like it has done her any harm
although she'll probably need a few weekends at Esalen
to straighten out her head.

Divina darling, I've come to free you.
But Divina's eyes are like stoned.
Has she been given a dog's brain already?

Oy, the fifteen minutes are up
and the whole pack of loonies burst in, grab us,
tie us up, and proceed with the operation.
There must be something to do, but it seems hopeless.

While the faithful Igor prepared the surgical instruments
and swung the great radiotrope into place
that directed the plastrons to the surgery,
the dwarf doctor took a great book off a bible-stand
and held it before us, turning the pages,
his eyes misty with memory:
"Here is my Book of the Dead," he said,
"the record of my experiments, my life work.
In the early stages I had such childish ideas,
that the serum could be made from blood and hair,
from flesh even." He riffled through
page after page of virgin sacrificed.
"But now I know it is a vibration one must catch.
I have the secret at last and tonight
I will finish my work: We will have the serum."

Madame Imperia could not resist giving a triumphant shriek.
"You mean," I said, "there will be no sacrifice of life?"
"No, she shall be alive and well...well, almost...."
Here the mad dwarf faltered.
We strained at the bonds desperately. "What do you mean?"
"She will lack her...ah...her organ of generation."
"You mean you are taking out her cunt, you creep?" We blurted.
"A trifle. She'll be otherwise perfect.
My wife will be beautiful again after a few well-placed injections,
and I'll be free to go back to my original interest,
the study of the generative cycle of the four-toed wallaby."
The monster! Now I was really mad.
With my tongue I pried off the false cap of my right molar
putting into action a radio transmitter.
By clicking the teeth in Morse code
messages could be sent.
"Isle of Dead mission calling Headquarters," I clicked.
I must have looked like I had a severe case of the chatters.
"Send choppers in at once."
Meanwhile the doctor continued with his work
zeroing the radiotrope right into target.
There was no time to wait for helicopters, troops, Medicaid—
I had to act.
There was an emergency capsule in one of my left molars—
I broke it out and swallowed.
It contained a special drug
to give five minutes of superhuman strength
but it had to be used with caution
because immediately after that you passed out.
I had to take care of this situation in five minutes—or else.
The drug coursed through my veins, my chest swelled,
I felt like superman to the rescue.
I snapped my bonds easily,
took Igor by the throat with one hand,
and Dr. Cranshaw with the other,
and tied them like a big sandwich
with Madame Imperia in between clawing at them both,
as the pack of dogmen ran howling into the woods.

Of course I pulled the plug on the equipment at once.
And there was my Divina lying on the operating table,
her breasts bulging up at me, her eyes and wet lips
imploring me to come to her,
and with the superman drug in my veins
I had supersex to give her:
I felt it throbbing up in my loins.
That would bring her to her senses again if anything would.
When she saw the size of it she screamed,
then her brain clicked off, her eyes glazed,
and she started panting.
Give it to me, she moaned,
and ground her hips up as far as the thongs allowed her.
It's all for you baby, I said, and reached out
but she seemed to be getting further away from me.
I took bigger steps, but got slower and slower,
the earth whirled
and I slipped off into darkness.

When I awoke I was back at the stationhouse
on a couch in the locker room
and the Chief was leaning over me giving me a hand job saying,
Boy, you really need it bad.
I groaned and pushed him away.
Did you get Cranshaw and the others?

They're all behind bars
and we've got the dogcatcher rounding up the dogmen.
We hope to place them in good homes.
Divina has already made an application for a couple of them.

Where's Divina, Boss? Were we too late?

She'll be better than ever, Sonny,
once her cunt cools off.
The doc is putting ice cubes up it.

And Madame Imperia?

She completely flipped out I'm afraid,
but you know, it's a mystery to me
because in the struggle to get a hold of her
her mask ripped off
and there was nothing wrong with her.
In fact, she was a darn good-looking dame.

Then the doctor must have discovered the serum
but they were too crazy already
to know they had succeeded.
That book of his must be worth a fortune.

You mean the book he was raving about,
his Book of the Dead?

Yes, get it and put it under lock and key.
We're going to be on easy street.

Oh shit, Sonny, I guess I didn't tell you.
There was a little fire—or rather a big one—
and the whole joint burned down—
you know those old houses.

Then our only hope is the doctor.
He'll know the secret.

The doctor? He's completely nuts.

Then I'd advise giving him a little laboratory to play around in
in the nuthouse, and a free hand
to experiment on the inmates
and a big book to write in.
I'll bet Revlon will finance the whole thing.

Just as the Chief turned back to his dirty picture book
with his hand stealing fondly into his open fly
the phone rang and he picked it up:
"What the hell you say? A thing? What kind of thing?

You say this thing came out of a lab at Caltech
when the chemicals were all spilled during the earthquake
and has been what? Eating co-eds
and getting bigger and bigger?
I thought it was a boys' school?
Oh, Women's Lib had a demonstration there and things changed....
I'll send my man right over to investigate.
Yeah, he's the one who cracked the Cranshaw case.

So there went my vacation. I was on a new case,
one that would prove to be the toughest in my career,
fighting an extra-terrestrial blob
that made people into zombies...
but that's another story.

To Ganapati, Hindu God of Auspiciousness

A domestic god seems to be running things lately
and the gods of public life, glamour, and art
have gone on to those who want them.

Mine is the god of golden hands, four of them,
who sets me to fixing, building, cooking, and cleaning.
I cut hair, serve meals, grow plants, sew pants.

The plants smile at me while drying up from steam heat,
the food sings to me from the frying pan,
the chair I repair trembles and sighs.

I have served under other gods:
The baboon made me universal sex slave
and under the crocodile I made the literary scene.
With the Roarer, lion god, I tried to save the world.

Now I pray only to Ganapati
with his friendly elephant's head, humor in his eyes,
and four hands to deal lucky cards with.

But I see a time coming, and soon,
when I have to get a job unless you, dear elephant,
save me by fiddling with my horoscope.
Do you see a Ford fellowship in my future?

Well, I will pray for that divine aid when I must.
Now the radiators are puffing
and I can sit at my desk near the bed
spread with the colors of Morocco.

There's plenty of time later for ambition
or if not, so what, I don't feel like it anyway.
May these auspicious times continue, Ganapati,
just keep the wolf from my door.

68

Plant Poems

1

As the leading agronomist
in the Kharkov Agricultural
Institute
I want to announce the discovery
that plants feel as we do
but since they cannot talk
they are considered insensible.

Actually they do make sounds
but on a different wavelength
than our ears can hear
and when you chop up a lettuce
it is saying Ouch.

2

I once had a plant on my windowsill
that grew down the outside of the building in summer.
It was all leaves at my end where I watered it
(that plant drank tons of water),
but visiting the people in the apartment below one day
I saw it blooming in their window.

3

When I bring water into the room
the plants start sending out
tremors of excitement
that water produces on their senses.

Like your cat rubs against your legs
talking out loud
while you open the can of catfood

4

My apartment is shabby really
but especially at night in lamplight it glows.
It's the plants that do that.

Plants are beings of great richness.
Of course they must be tended faithfully like pets
or like a monster child that will never grow up
but stay home with you always
and have to be fed and looked after.

I never understand the tragedy of an idiot child:
People don't mind having a dog around the house to love.
Well that kind of child is the same thing.
It doesn't go to school or on dates or get a job.
That is no more in its nature
than for plants to bark or make a mess
(bless you, green ones, for that)
but what a glow they bring to every room.

Jellyfish Invasion

each jellyfish being a colony
of cooperating organisms
it is amazing that one
is so much like another
like greek city states scattered
over the unruly land
some of the little creatures
play kidneys and others
are good for hearts
okay everybody join hands
and sing the national anthem

there must have been a time
when things were looser
a time between gas and solid
when things could shift about
imagine seeing through people
or whatever we were then
and hugging vapor to vapor
or jelly to jelly
that was an inventive time
this whole earth a big glob
and everyone shifting sex like mad
according to circumstance
and trying out different shapes like hats
lets get together and be dinosaurs gang
we do it now
but its like a tree trunk
trying to take a walk
better stay home
there are some things decided on

even the jellyfish is decided
each one has a constitution by plato
no poets wanted

this week a whole flock
sailed into riis park and the rockaways
like greeks in long ships
and won back the waters from the swimmers
troy fell and the trojans
fled screaming

Toothy Lurkers

The shores are patrolled by sharks,
east coast and west alike,
Don't look, they're there all right—

better squeeze shut your eyes
as you dunk yourself
in the sharky sea.

Right now my greatest fear
is to wake up and find myself
floating with bare toes.

How do surfers dare
go so far out
with those toothy lurkers in the waves?

Giant Pacific Octopus

I live with a giant pacific octopus:
He settles himself down beside me on the couch in the evening.
With two arms he holds a book
that he reads with his single eye:
He wears a pair of glasses over it for reading.

Two more arms go walking over to the sideboard across the room
where the crackers and cheese spread he loves are,
and they send back endless canapés, like a conveyor belt.

While his mouth is drooling and chomping,
another arm comes over and gropes me lightly:
It is like a breeze on my balls, that sweet tentacle.

Other arms start slipping around my body under my clothes,
they wiggle right in, one around my waist,
and all over, and down the crack of my ass.

I am drawn into his midst where his hot mouth waits for kisses
and I kiss him and make him into a boy
as all giant pacific octopuses are really
when you take them into your arms.

All their arms fluttering around you
become everywhere sensations of pleasure.
So, his sweet eye looks at me and his little mouth kisses me
and I swear he has the body of a greek god,
my giant pacific octopus boychik.

So this was what was in store
when I first saw him in the aquarium
huddled miserably on the rock
ignoring the feast of live crabs
they put in his windowed swimming pool.

You take home a creature like that, who needs love,
who is a mess when you meet
but who can open up like a flower with petal arms waving
    around—a beauty—
and it is a total pleasure to have him around,
even collapsible as he is like a big toy,
for as long as he will stay, one night or a lifetime,
for as long as god will let you have him.

Three Views of Eden:

1. The Expulsion

When last seen he was in a garden
frisking with the creatures and the plants.
He almost preferred the plants nowadays
with their stillness that never exhausted you
but somehow pumped you full of good air.

We drew a curtain of privacy over his life then
for even he has a right to a private life,
for a while anyway, although you know as well as I
that the world was going to call him again.
Some people are really public and he's one of them:

He'll have to come out of that garden he so loves
and step into the streets and join the throng
hurrying down to the central marketplace
where a throne and a gallows will be set up.
He'll be chosen, as his fate demands,
for one or the other, but never know which
until the trapdoor falls or the crown descends.

2. Exile

Going out of my garden into the world of strangers
I don't ask for a great god's help,
I only ask a little one,
say the god of stones.

But invoking the small god
you risk intervention by a greater,
whether you want all that thunder and lightning or not.
Leave us in peace, great ones,
don't make us act out your cosmic dramas in our lives.

Why should we suffer that way
when all around us are the little gods, playful and ingenious,

a lot easier to live with than the roarers
who make us feel divine one minute
and rotten the whole rest of the year.

The trouble is that the shape of a small god
is a place a larger god can live in if he wants to.
But why should great Yahweh, bigshot,
crawl into my beloved god of stones
stretching his little face all awry
as he looms up into the heavens and darkens the sea
frightening some children playing on a lonely shore
who look up at his monster cloudshapes in the sky?

What choice have we got? None.
Life has put me out of my garden. I go.
Comfort me, stones.
Leaves like lips, speak to me.
Bug, let's race. You win darling.
Thank you little ones for the sweet moments.

Well, if great Yahweh descends
I have to don my hat and prayer shawl for him.

3. No to Eden

Eden was a garden all right
but none of my feelings had emerged yet
so it was like a book I was too young for.
There was no question of pleasure:
I even remember it as painful.
It was not the fruit of a tree that changed me then,
or rather it was all the fruits and flowers.
It was no snake alone,
but all the creatures were pointing in that direction:

I just never dreamed that it applied to me too.
But buds form and open in us like eyes
and suddenly different behavior is possible.

Why didn't that ever occur to me before, I thought,
and got up and walked away.

Everybody is like that, aren't they?
Even if we face failure and pain, we go;
we'd go in spite of everything.
The garden is stifling, that paradise,
and we go forth with vague heroic ideas
of fighting battles and winning the world.

We discover of course that we had it all wrong,
that life is very long as it races by,
that everything we vowed we'd never do, we do.
We have grown in the seven directions of the soul
and none of it is to be judged.

How simple life was before in the garden limits:
We sat in the sun and felt good,
it rained and we cried,
but we didn't have any choice in the matter.
Now we ache to see naked people,
on cold days sit in a hot bath for hours.
Can we raise the unlikely question,
Would I go back if I could?
Still I answer, No, to Eden.

The Tailspin

Going into a tailspin
in those days meant curtains.
No matter how hard you pulled back on the stick
the nose of the plane wouldn't come up.

Spinning round, headed for a target of earth,
the whine of death in the wing struts,
instinct made you try to pull out of it that way, by force,
and for years aviators spiraled down and crashed.

Who could have dreamed that the solution
to this dreaded aeronautical problem
was so simple?
Every student flier learns this nowadays:
You move the joystick in the direction of the spin
and like a miracle the plane stops turning
and you are in control again
to pull the nose up out of the dive.

In panic we want to push the stick away from the spin,
wrestle the plane out of it,
but the trick is, as in everything,
to go with the turning willingly,
rather than fight, give in, go with it,
and that way come out of your tailspin whole.

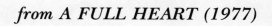

from A FULL HEART (1977)

New York

I live in a beautiful place, a city
people claim to be astonished
when you say you live there.
They talk of junkies, muggings, dirt, and noise,
missing the point completely.

I tell them where they live it is hell,
a land of frozen people.
They never think of people.

Home, I am astonished by this environment
that is also a form of nature
like those paradises of trees and grass

but this is a people paradise
where we are the creatures mostly,
though thank God for dogs, cats, sparrows, and roaches.

This vertical place is no more an accident
than the Himalayas are.
The city needs all those tall buildings
to contain the tremendous energy here.
The landscape is in a state of balance.
We do God's will whether we know it or not:
Where I live the streets end in a river of sunlight.

Nowhere else in the country do people
show just what they feel—
we don't put on any act.
Look at the way New Yorkers
walk down the street. It says,
I don't care. What nerve,
to dare to live their dreams, or nightmares,
and no one bothers to look.

True, you have to be an expert to live here.
Part of the trick is not to go anywhere, lounge about,
go slowly in the midst of the rush for novelty.
Anyway, besides the eats the big event here
is the streets, which are full of love—
we hug and kiss a lot. You can't say that
for anywhere else around. For some
it's a carnival of sex—
there's all the opportunity in the world.
For me it is no different:
Out walking, my soul seeks its food.
It knows what it wants.
Instantly it recognizes its mate, our eyes meet,
and our beings exchange a vital energy,
the universe goes on Charge
and we pass by without holding.

A Full Heart

My mother's family was made up of loving women.
They were, on the whole, bearers,
though Esther, the rich sister, had only one,
she was the exception.

Sarah, the oldest, had five with her first husband
(that was still in Poland),
was widowed and came here
where she married a man with four of his own,
and together they had another five,
all of whom she raised, feeding them in relays,
except little Tillie who sat in the kitchen
and ate with everyone, meaning all the time,
resulting in a fat figure
that made her despair of ever finding a husband,
but miraculously she did,
for God has decreed there is someone for everyone,
if you're desperate enough
and will take what you can get.

Aunt Rachel had twelve, raising them in a stable.
She was married to a junk dealer
who kept horses to haul the wagons.
He was famous for his stinginess
so they lived in a shack surrounded by bales of hay.
That was in America, in a slum called Bronzeville
that the black people have now inherited from the Jews,
God help them.
Then, as now, plenty of kids turned out bad,
going to work for that Jewish firm, Murder Incorporated,
or becoming junkies like one of my cousins did.

My mother had only six
but that's not counting...I'll say no more
than she was always pregnant,

with a fatalistic "What can you do?"
("Plenty," her friend Blanche replied—she was liberated.
"You don't have to breed like a rabbit.")
Like her mother who had a baby a year in Poland
until Grandpa left for America
giving her a rest.
There were women who kept bearing
even then, mysteriously, as from habit.

Women were always tired in those days and no wonder,
with the broken-down bodies they had
and their guts collapsed,
for with every child they got a dragging down.
My mother finally had hers
tied back up in the hospital and at the same time
they tied those over-fertile tubes,
which freed her from "God's terrible curse on women."

And not just the bearing, but the work:
The pots couldn't be big enough for those hungry broods—
Sarah used hospital pots for hers.
And then the problem of filling the pots,
getting up at dawn to go to the fishing boats
for huge fish carcasses cheap,
buying bushels of half-spoiled vegetables for pennies,
begging the butcher for bones,
and then lugging it all home on their bad legs.
They didn't think of their looks for a minute,
and better they didn't, shapeless as that life made them.
(And yet they remained attractive to their men,
by the evidence of their repeated pregnancies.)
They just went around wrecks, always depressed,
unable to cope, or hiding in bed
while the children screamed.
"Escape, escape, there must be escape"
was my mother's theme song, until at last
her children escaped from her and her misery,

having wrecked her life, that endless sacrifice,
for what?

I see the proletarian women like them on the streets,
cows with udders to the waist
lugging black oilcloth shopping bags,
the mamales, the mamacitas, the mammies,
the breeders of the world with loving eyes.
They sit around the kitchen table with full hearts
telling each other their troubles—
never enough money, the beasts their men were to them,
the sorrow life was for a woman, a mother,
the children turning out no good—
and fed each other pieces of leftover meat from the icebox
to make up a little for life's pain
and sighing, drank tea
and ate good bread and butter.

Roaches

An old decrepit city like London
doesn't have any.
They ought to love it there
in those smelly, elegant buildings.
Surely I myself have smuggled some in in my luggage
but they obviously don't like the English—
for that alone I should love them.

They are among the brightest
and most attractive of small creatures
though you have to be prepared
for the look of horror
on the faces of out-of-town guests
when a large roach walks across the floor
as you are sipping drinks.
You reach out and swat,
and keeping the conversation going
pick up the corpse and drop it into an ashtray
feeling very New Yorky doing it.
After all, you've got to be tough to live here—
the visitor didn't make it.

Roaches also thrive on it here:
They set up lively communes
in open boxes of rice, spaghetti, and matzohs.
You come in to make coffee in the morning
and find a dead one floating in the kettle
and dots of roach shit on the dishes,
hinting at roachy revels the night before.

If you let them alone
they stop running at the sight of you
and whisker about
taking a certain interest in whatever you are doing,
and the little ones, expecting like all babies to be adored,

frolic innocently in the sink,
even in daytime when grownup roaches rest
after a night of swarming around the garbage bag.
The trouble with this approach is
they outbreed you and take over,
even moving sociably right into your bed.

Which brings up the question, Do they bite?
Some say yes, and if yes,
do they carry Oriental diseases?
Even though you have tried to accept them
there comes a point when you find your eyes
studying labels of roach killers on supermarket shelves,
decide to try a minimal approach, buy one,
but when you attack with spray can aimed
they quickly learn to flee.
The fastest of course live to multiply
so they get cleverer all the time
with kamikaze leaping into space,
or zigzagging away,
race into far corners of the apartment
where they drop egg-sacs in their last throes
to start ineradicable new colonies.

When you light the oven
they come out and dance on the hot stove top
clinging with the tips of their toes,
surviving by quick footwork until you swat them.
Or if you spray it first
you have the smell of roaches roasting slowly.

And when you wash them down the drain
without their being certifiably dead
do they crawl up when the coast is clear?
Some even survive the deadliest poisons devised by man
and you have weird, white mutations running about.
Dying, they climb the walls, or up your legs, in agony,

making you feel like a dirty rat,
until they fall upside down with frail legs
waving in the air.

No more half-measures—
it's them or us you finally realize
and decide on nothing less than total fumigation:
The man comes while you are out
and you return to a silent apartment, blissfully roach-free.
You vacuum up the scattered bodies of the unlucky,
pushing down guilty feelings, lonely feelings,
and congratulate yourself.

                You booby,
they have only moved over to the neighbor's
who is now also forced to fumigate,
and just when you are on the princess phone crowing to your friends,
back they come, the whole tribe of them,
many gone now
due to their trivial life span and chemical adversaries
but more numerous than ever with the newborn
and all the relatives from next door and the neighborhood with them,
you standing there outraged, but secretly relieved
as they swarm into the kitchen from every crevice,
glad to be home, the eternal innocents,
greeting you joyfully.

The Reservoir

The ancient reservoir,
an underground lake beneath the city,
has been closed to the public by the government
due to stringent budget cuts.

The news fills me with dismay.
It was the only thing I cared about
in that city of minarets, domes, and ruined palaces.
And to think I could have seen it
but passed it by, dismissing it
as a minor tourist attraction, not worth
spending fifteen minutes or fifty cents on.

I suppose there was nothing much to it:
You could go out on it in a boat,
though never all the way—it has never been fully explored.
Imagine a city having a source of sweet water under it,
not needing aqueducts or to use the polluted river.

And maybe even it was a city underground,
now flooded, as the sewers of modern Jerusalem
once were Roman streets.

Too late I realize it was one of the important things.

It was closed for centuries
before being rediscovered and opened again.
And even if the population
never thought or even knew about it
still its presence must have affected them.
Like a desert is an energy accumulator,
a mountain a magnetic pole,
bodies of water give off an exciting influence.

Now it is shut again
and those carved pillars of limestone
that stretch away into the gloom
may collapse and the whole thing fill up with garbage,
become a sewer instead of a reservoir,
that underground lake, sacred to dervishes,
lost track of, and profaned.

And for how long, O my people,
I cry from the bottom of my wretched heart,
will it still be possible to reopen it, and explore?

The Gods Desert Antony

after Cavafy

I stand by my window looking over this valley.
    There is a sad music in the air
for when the gods desert you
    they play a music that we feel as grief.
Antony heard it too one night in Alexandria
    when he was king, and for queen
    he had Cleopatra, that delicious woman,
    as I had you, dear one.
What a city that was to be king of.
Then he heard the music of those rascally gods
    masquerading as a band of minstrels
    as those wise ones, those friends, foretold.
And at that moment, did he weep?
    Did he rage at the gods
    for depriving him of such a paradise?
Yes, he wept, he raged,
for you do not give up all that
    without tears and cursing.
You do not act noble, standing on the hill
    outside the city
    and wave goodbye to the Alexandria you are losing.
No, you tear your clothes in mourning
    and go wailing through the world, alone,
alone forever perhaps, forever probably,
    and never forgive, certainly never forget,
for the kingdom had become your soul
    and without it now you are nothing.

Kabul, 1971

The Lost, Dancing

after Cavafy

When the drums come to your door
do not try to shut them out,
do not turn away and resist them,
for they have come to tell you what you need to hear,
they are your fate.
When Antony heard them
he knew then that he had lost Egypt forever.
He did not shriek or tear his clothes
for he always knew they would come someday.
What the drums speak to you
is so inevitable you have to agree with them—
nothing else could be right.
So when the drummers and dancers come to your door
your life changes,
and with no bitterness
but with a sad smile
—after all what you had you had,
you loved the way few men love—
and as someone who was worthy of such a kingdom,
join the army of the lost, dancing,
follow the drums
and turn and wave goodbye
to the Alexandria you are losing.

Rio de Janeiro
Carnival, 1974

94

The Book of Sorrow

This notebook, empty.
What shall be written in it?
It is waiting for the words of pain,
the life to come without my dear one.
The record of a wanderer without a home.
So many pages and each
a day of loneliness.
How long can this go on?
After this book is filled
there will be another, and another,
and another....
The story of my life.

Gone Blind

He's a shrine, my blind friend at home.
Wherever I go, and I go far,
I remember him, and my heart is full.

Always he fills me with feeling
like someone far from home
who longs for his mother.

In his blindness I am at home
for I find in it my fullness.
In his helplessness—
and he is not practically helpless
but helpless as we all are,
to help ourselves—
my life becomes a frailty.

O to be there,
to put my arms around his sightlessness—
He has become so gentle now,
all arrogance gone
of one who makes demands on life.
In his gratitude for love
he shines with love.
In his victimhood he shines
like babies shine,
like women shine from their pain,
like saints and animals shine.

That he is not here with me is unthinkable.
Where have I lost him? Why is he not here?
O he is, here, in my heart.
He is my sacred figure, a shrine.

Gone blind
he has brought me light.

Living with an Aries

They want to run away constantly—
this you must discourage,
but luckily they are easily discouraged by delay
for their nature is to act instantly
or their energies die.

They love little harmless lies invented on the instant
though the truth would do as well.
Indulge them in this. Resist correcting
the exaggerated versions of stories they tell,
or saying "we" which wrecks
the free-wheeling image they like to project.

They are ready for a love affair
every two weeks.
Pity their discarded lovers
and be glad you are just in the friend category:
You will last.
You can discourage them in their romantic fallacies
by criticism or better, ridicule.

The trouble is they live or they die
and there is no in-between.
Their ambitious plans can succeed amazingly
if they act at once, on the instant of conception,
or fail, but the important thing is
they live by action.

Nothing, nothing is more pitiful
than a crushed Aries, or a caged one.
Possess one to your peril, and theirs.
Don't be fooled by placidity:
Underneath is a volcano, ready to blow its stack.
If it doesn't, they develop alarming diseases
that only the movies could invent,

but on the brink of death
will recover miraculously—
teaching their would-be keepers
to let go, be content to look on
their mad head-on scramble for doing,
for a kind of life
anyone else would consider hell on earth
but which suits their natures.

How often can you batter a wall with your head
and live? You reason with them.
No use, they will continue
until one or the other gives.

So if you love, stand back and let them.
Your only consolation is this:
They will come to you for comfort at the end.

Visiting Home

I

It is an exercise in independence
not being like them.

Seeing that our bodies
are of the same nature
I religiously do my yoga
and stay open to other possibilities.

I remind myself I am allowed to shit.
So far I've been able to
though this morning I doubted.

Genital feelings nevertheless
are a long ways off.
They still have me by the balls.

My father and I suffer the same ailments:
electric leg in the night, after back trouble,
prima donna stomach,
a ringing in the left ear.

My mother declares her goal
is not to have to do anything
(that's me too)
and she refuses to make any effort
even to save her life.

We suggest activities
but all she wants is to go away on a Greyhound bus,
live in hotels
and hang out in the lobby and cocktail lounge
talking to people.
Old ladies ought to be allowed.

I too am a roamer,
a talker with strangers,
but I have stars for travel
and she's stuck at home.

The trouble is she's one of the poor.
My father holds the purse strings
and it's as if he were still doling out to her
the daily allowance of five dollars
to feed the family on.
She will always believe in revolution
and be a feminist through and through.

By studying them
can I really know anything about myself?
But I can't stop.
Oh, all this concentrating for years
on what happened in childhood
to make me a mess,
all the analysis of transferences and dreams
to see how I repeat the defeat. . . .
All that rebellion against being like them.

II

At lunch my father sits
hunched over his food
like some incredibly primitive
prehistoric man.

His face I feel as an unused
structure within my own. It is made
for glaring, raging, judging, criticizing.
I wish I could melt it down softer.

Under my mild looks
I have his skull, his features,

even his expression,
afraid of life, afraid of the flow.

We share an essential joylessness.
As I get older, that is starting to show
and it is a measure of our difficulties
that I will hate looking like him.

At the table he will hardly meet my eyes.
His slide away, masking a confusion of feelings.
Yet when I say I am going to leave
he gets a stricken look.

My mother shyly kisses me
half on the lips. It is sweet.
I think of my grandmother's huge soft wet kisses,
messages from another world of feeling
where nothing is held back.

My mother's eyes are wide open.
We gaze at each other and love flows.
My father and I can't seem to find a way
to let that happen.

What if I said to him, Daddy—
though it would be better in Yiddish,
the language he can express himself in—
Daddy, I don't want to go on for the rest of my life
with this barrier between us.

I don't blame you for the past,
my hellish childhood, and the years after,
that nightmare, when I didn't know how to live my life.
Let's try to be straight with each other,
though there is no ignoring the wreckage between us.

But it is as if I were waiting for him to start,
as though he alone had the key to that door

to what feels like the possibility of . . . of what?
a better life? a rootedness?
Making a vital connection it is hard to live without
to be whole.

III

Before I was born he took the first step
in our estrangement
by changing his name from Feldman to Field
although even Feldman wasn't his name
(though he made Field mine).
In Europe it was Felscher
but at Immigration they wrote down Feldman.
And what's the difference,
wasn't that a good Jewish name?

As we came, he named us like lords and ladies:
Adele, Alice, Edward, Richard, Robert, and Barbara,
and moved as far from the Lower East Side as he could
to a town in the Anglo-Saxon Protestant world,
the real America.
He did not have to cope much with that,
as we did every day.
He went to work in the city
where, with his new name,
he was able to go into advertising,
at that time practically closed to Jews.
He couldn't talk to those people, or us
without stammering, or yelling.

He did not want to know
we hated the house, the block, the village
where the people didn't want us—
after all, that was his achievement in life.
The family was his world and he wanted it to be ours
and not adopt the alien ways around us.

He avoided the relatives from the old country—
even our grandparents we hardly knew.
He felt superior to them all.
We ate on Yom Kippur, though he didn't,
having a stomachache every year,
and mixed milk with meat,
though he drew the line at Christmas trees.

It wasn't even that he was trying not to be Jewish
but it was his way of being modern.
He and my mother spoke Yiddish together
but we never learned more
than the words for "don't hit him" or "to bed."
We were left out of the secret world
of their real identity.

When we asked about our religion
he said we were atheists, and we shocked everybody
by going around insisting on it.
But when we asked him our nationality
he said we were American Jews
which in our town just meant Jews.
And what does God have to do with it?
You don't need God to be a Jew.
Anyway, we were beaten up
whether we believed in God or not
for a Jew was automatically an atheist to them.
Or maybe we were beaten up
because everyone knew in those days before Israel
it was our role in life to be.

Some people once met in our house
discussing whether to convert for the sake of the children
to save us from the Nazis,
for surely what was happening in Germany
was possible where we lived
with the Bund meeting in the high schools

and swastikas painted all over—
but we knew nothing could be done
to make you anything but a Jew.
Change your name to Field
and they call you Fieldinsky.

There was a kind of native fascism there
where the people disliked everything darker,
everything foreign, races that bred fast,
with daughters developing large breasts early,
races that did not understand conformity
but stuck to what they were.

Everything closer to New York was inferior,
even girls living the next town nearer.
Speaking a foreign language was unthinkable
and having foreign parents unbearable.

They didn't like me and with good reason:
my long, hooked nose; kinky, black hair;
wrinkly skin on the back of my hands—
I was a small, skinny, dark, and dirty boy,
my prick was button-sized and circumcised,
my parents spoke Yiddish
and I had lots of sisters and brothers.
We were animals.

My father ignored everything.
He didn't want us to be like the townsfolk
but to be an enclave, a ghetto, with him the master.
He made rules. Many things were forbidden:
   to believe in God, heaven, angels, or ghosts—
      all superstitions;
   to listen to jazz or popular music—for the goyim—
      or chamber music, or Wagner or Sibelius—Nazis;
   to participate in school activities or sports—
      for the goyim who were not serious about life;

to care about your looks, clothes—
    tinsel, for the goyim;
to mind being different and want to be popular—
    contemptible;
and any evidence of sexuality was most forbidden—
    for bums.
In short, it was forbidden to have fun.
Duties around the house came first,
practicing music, and homework.

My parents made fun of everyone,
the neighbor who claimed to like opera,
the girl who wanted to be a movie star;
this one spent cultural evenings,
that one fell for the flattery of salesgirls and men;
above all anyone who was pleased with himself
or spent money on his pleasures;
and of course the goyim for their narrow, orderly lives.
All the relatives were torn to bits.

There's the main sin of Jewish parents,
being overcritical,
so you grow up ashamed of yourself, worthless
(if they don't love you you must be worthless),
more critical of yourself than anyone could ever be,
ridiculing what you long for, what you need to go on living,
ashamed to admit you want love, or anything,
and denying it to the end.
Even ashamed of being ashamed.

You dream only of running away.
My soul, but not my lips, cried out,
"Doesn't anyone want a little boy?"
But there was nobody out there
who would ever want someone like me,
who would ever take me in.

My father's theory of child-raising
was that it doesn't matter what you do to them, what
    they hear—
you feed them, clothe them, house them, and train them,
and they grow up adults,
that state of being grownup I could hardly wait for,
and by some magic all the terror and guilt
and self-loathing would go away.
Our sexuality would start to function
the way it was expected to,
and we would become famous.
Or more important,
we wouldn't do anything to shame him.

IV

Yiskidor, when he dies I won't know the Hebrew words to say.
Yiskidor, I won't be able to help the soul he doesn't believe in find rest.
Yiskidor, I go through life cut off from my ancestors.
Yiskidor, I live a life of shit.
Yiskidor, I'm a bum, I'm no man, I'm not even at the beginning.
Yiskidor, I don't know the prayers.
Yiskidor, I don't know the sacred rites.
Yiskidor, I buried my friend Alfred and it was done badly,
       nobody wailed, nobody tore their clothes—
       I didn't know you were supposed to,
       though somehow I felt like doing it.
Yiskidor, I took a clod of earth from the grave
       and have placed it in my shrine with his books
       and the letter from Jerusalem telling how he died
       of alcohol and drugs like a movie star,
       his dogs barking to alert the neighbors.
       He always reminded me of Marilyn Monroe—
       he had that ultimate glamour
       and went around in a cloud of admiration,
       though he never felt loved.
       Like a good Jew, he went to Jerusalem to die
       but his family brought him back

and buried him in Staten Island.
Yiskidor, when the clods hit the coffin I bawled
and everybody turned and stared at me.

Yiskidor, I pray for my mother every way I can
though I don't know the prayers to protect her.
Yiskidor, how she suffers, my mommeh.
I promised I would take her to California when I
grew up
and we'd live in a house overlooking the ocean,
just so she wouldn't suffer anymore.
Yiskidor, what is my sacred duty to my parents
but to honor them, both in life and in death,
for they produced me by the holy process,
Yiskidor, and if they fucked me up
they did not know what they were doing.

Yiskidor, and look what they gave me, the gifts,
my life's full of gifts, all my loves.
Yiskidor, for that little boy who didn't know it but was lucky,
with parents that made life hard,
Yiskidor, who complicated things for me
so I could never take the easy path
but had to choose my own
when all I wanted was to be standard:
straight hair, straight nose, straight.
Yiskidor, for that desperate wish I went to sleep with
every night,
"When I wake up I'll look right, be popular,
They'll like me."

Yiskidor, I woke up at last and they liked me
(even if I don't like myself)
so I don't read the "How to be Popular" books
anymore.
Now I read the "How to be Saved" books.
They all say, Awaken,

follow the path of the heart
which leads to the east.
There is no one to blame anymore
and what you become is up to you.

Yiskidor, and I believe them, I can't help it.
My family screams at me, Be skeptical.
I'd like to be but I can't.
Yiskidor, I see I had the perfect parents
for everything has turned out right
like a miracle.

Yiskidor, I had the illusion I could invent my Self,
I thought I could live by the rules of psychiatrists,
Yiskidor, I had the illusion I could get free of history,
not only our history, but my own history.
Yiskidor, but now I must go back to the beginning
if I can find it. It is surely somewhere
inside myself, still trapped
in that defeat at the first breath
when I understood my predicament—
which I chose.

Yiskidor, they have my love, the dear ones who are old now.
Yiskidor, all men and women are my brothers and sisters now.
Yiskidor, how I love men, now that I have dared
to look in their eyes
and stand my ground as the energies connect.
Yiskidor, if men would reach out and hold each other
they would know we are all brothers.
Yiskidor, I am my father's son, God help me.
Yiskidor, I am my father's son, the heir
to the mess he couldn't solve.
Yiskidor, thank God I am my mother's son too
for what she gave me
is what I survived by.
I cry Mamma, and am healed.
Yiskidor, I am my father's son.
Even if I can't stand it, still
I am.

Sharks

Especially at evening
everyone knows the sharks come in
when the sun makes puddles of blood on the sea
and the shadows darken.

It is then, as night comes on
the sharks of deep water
approach the shore
and beware, beware, the late swimmer.

from THE CRIER (New Poems)

"I can't stand a crier." —Eda Lioi

"Actor cries buckets,
    audience sleeps.
Hold back your tears
    and audience weeps." —Vera Soloviova

"Zu hab rachmones vor sich allein,
der beste weg gesindt zu sein." —Yiddish proverb

The Crier

As much as I'd like to be
a jolly, fat old man,
skinny I remain
no matter what I eat,

and jolly I'll never become—
though I perfectly understand
the reasons for that, the same
as prevent me from getting fat.

But if I go on living,
unlikely as it seems
with signs of doom in my hand
and symptoms multiplying,

I can't think of anything
that I would rather do
than spend my old age crying—
if they allow me to.

Over Fifty

It wasn't until I was over fifty that I started to understand
life is divided into two parts,
and no more young, I saw I was in the half now
that included the retired, the feeble and wornout, inmates
of nursing homes and prostate, colostomy, and senility wards—
in short, THE WORLD OF THE OLD and all that means
rather than THE WORLD OF YOUTH the whole world celebrates.
It's enough to make one grumpy
if not be cause for trembling—it's clear
these are the last days of my life.

Not that there aren't survivors—
let's not ask for looks, but with luck
some keep mind and spirit,
though that's no consolation when you walk
through the sex bazaar of the streets
unwanted and ignored—a zero.

Most people in my half of life are like ships
floundering in a gale with hatches warped,
valves stuck and everything leaking. Now and then
one sinks fast and is never seen again—
a lot are going down these days.
Already I can see that nothing
is going to work right for long—
the warping, sticking, and leaking has begun
and it does no good to complain to doctors:
What can you expect, old boy, they say—
you're over fifty.

Of course, most of the body still works fine
but that's not what you die of—
it's from the one thing that doesn't
even if all the rest is perfect.
But dying's another question, and just now

114

it's not HOW TO DIE, but HOW TO LIVE until then
that drives me nightly, no matter how tired,
to my exercises, designed to ward off disaster
one more day—the motive, pure terror.
Nascent mathematician, I find myself subtracting
every time the age is given in an obituary,
and I've suddenly become proprietor of a body
with a whole new set of problems.
Perhaps like in every other stage of life
they aren't solved, you just leave them behind—
except for the number one problem, How to Be Loved.

Far off now seem Being Popular and What to Be
When I Grow Up, and grown up,
What to Do with My Life, and above all,
How to Cope with the Insatiable Demands and Complications
of Sex, which always seemed the answer to meaninglessness,
the solution for feeling unwanted,
and the best excuse for not getting a job—

though the more I tried to make sex THE SOLUTION
the more miserably it failed, until the time came, O my friends,
when desire that once needed to be restrained
needed encouragement, and in fact became recreational—
or anyway, rather than a sex-fiend obsession,
whatever it is now it's not crucial to going on.

Like quitting smoking, that leaves
a lot more time on your hands,
though with time, as Berryman said, "rushing like a madman forward,"
there's nowhere to stop and think it all over.

This is an entirely different thing than life prepares you for,
nor are there any instructions for what's ahead.

Mirror Songs

1.

When you look, fierce face, in the mirror mornings
is it absolutely necessary to groan?
It's not that you're ugly really, just old and ravaged
with, wouldn't you say, haunted eyes?
Well, you alone know what they've seen.

If your life has turned you into this, remember,
you've worked hard not to make it even worse.
Think of all the talking and screaming
therapies you've tried, not to mention acupuncture,
diet cures, years of yoga exercises,
and, as good as anything really, prayer.

Instead of hating your face, shmeggege,
can't you dredge up the least compassion
for what you've gone through? Tenderness, perhaps?
Don't scorn yourself. Give yourself a medal, pops—
it's been a long haul out of the pits, if you are out yet,
and you look it.

2.

It takes nerve to live with hair like mine,
a Jewish frizz that defies the orthodoxy of goyish straight.
Some days, feeling shy, I groan
to see it, or what's left of it, in the mirror,
springing out around my gorgon head,
a giveaway, an impudence I'm not up to—
never to be standard, like the popular kids....

Tame it with scissors, comb, and oil,
inner voices say, and for years I obeyed.
Cut short and pasted down it's a dimension less,
easier to live with and the world approves.

But is it me, the real me? Fuck you all,
don't I have the right to be beautiful?

3.

It's in the bathroom that I loudly groan
        over my incandescent foolishness—

when I think of what I've said and done,
especially tonight at the dinner table. . . .
        O why did I have to blab like that
among those grown-up people?

You are a jerk and never will be other,
and right thou art to know thy estimate:
        It's written all over your silly face,

and therefore, you may well invoke
        the eternal fraternal principle,
a cry resounding down the ages

        to Gods and man alike,
        from Job to Christ-on-the-Cross to you:

O Brother!

4.

If today I am haggard and old
I've got no right to complain—
all through the years I was told
that I looked much younger than
I had any right to be.
I heard it again and again
but it meant less than nothing to me.
The unhappy youth I was then
in the dark pit of distress
couldn't take advantage of

that much-praised youthfulness
or any of the generous
(it now seems) offers of love—
none of that meant a thing.
And what also has to be faced
is if youth was a waste
it wasn't fate's but my own doing.

The Night Runners

Before Wolfetta drank the potion
that made her human so she could marry the Prince,
the witch warned her of the danger, the nights
she'd lie awake listening as her old pack
roamed the deserted streets of the capital.
And as predicted, Wolfetta lay there,
unable to keep her incisors from dripping saliva.
Mornings over their intimate breakfasts,
the Prince would be solicitous about her eye bags.

She'd been dealt a good hand by life—
the early years as a bitch with the pick of the pack,
and later with a Prince every woman had a yen for—
yes, everything, but . . . that howling in the night
as the Prince slept innocently beside her.
Her wolf heart was a tender one as wolf hearts are,
but teeth and nails on edge, she couldn't help drooling
at the pulsing vein in his throat . . . . One gash
and she could throw off human guise, join the night runners—
she shuddered, gripping the bedpost, but in her sleep
she tore the sheets to ribbons.

You pay a price for everything, she told herself—
like the mermaid the witch gave legs to
that, dancing with her lover, hurt like hell
and bled all over the ballroom,
but the penalty for changing her mind and going back to sea
was turning to foam and spray. The witch only cackled
when Wolfetta asked what would happen if she herself
again gave in to the old wolf call in the night.

The years passed, her profile coarsened, romance died.
The Prince no longer mounted her wolf-style as she taught him,
not that he was ever much good at it. One crystal night
when the pack seemed almost at the palace gates

she could no longer stand it, and into the throat
of her beloved bit, drank blood again and answered
the yipping of the pack with her nose to the moon.
Wind riffled her neck fur and her claws gripped the earth
deliciously like the old days, as she raced toward them.
Far off, the wolf dogs smelled on her the Prince's blood
and her own smell, almost human now,
and in the clearing in a circle stood,
eyes glittering, hackles raised,
until the old bitch, moaning
with the stored-up passion of her wasted human years
hurled herself among them in her grizzled fur....

The pack first tore her to bits,
then devoured every shred of her.

Too Late?

How hard I tried to be hard,
    to be arrogant and strong
like all those men I admired
    to whom I could never belong.

But, ah, friend, life is a breaker of backs
and from the dark balcony, on a movie screen in my head
I look at the youth I was then
who wouldn't be kissed and who wouldn't kiss,
and had not even begun to face his worthlessness,

and scorning as sissy all softness
as the years went rushing by,
crushed the longings of my sentimental heart.

The Irritant

in memoriam Walter Weiss

In the How-to-Cope-Brilliantly-in-the-End category,
a friend who died of a heart attack in his seventies:

Unlike other old men he was always able
to fill his life with new friends,
fearlessly talking to strangers,
even hitchhiking to make contact—
cops in patrol cars tried to discourage this
but ended up driving him home and taking his phone number.

He offered help with all problems,
setting himself up as an expert and applying a nutty analysis,
as good as anything, I guess.
He knew it was the attention that mattered—
everyone responds to that kind of flattery.

In asking directions, his trick
was to turn left if told to go right,
doing the opposite because it led
to complications, conversations, unexpected friends—
as a wise man once said, If everyone runs, you walk,
and if they go on feet, go on hands.

He never forgot that sex was the friendliest of gestures,
an overture to the desired Being-Together-a-Lot,
his dick the consolation prize
for all the young men who needed to be consoled.
He also used his money as necessary, and why not?
It's one of the sure-fire attractions.
How many men his age
have a handsome bevy of boys around,
even for free dinners?
Maybe it was hormones that accounted for his success,
because they certainly responded

to this smelly old man with a big dangle
offering free massage and advice
and were willing to let him take over their lives.

Toward the end, though, heart trouble
led him to doctors who advised
he'd not only have to change his ways
and accept a fixed invalidism, but also
take heart pills almost guaranteed
to make him impotent—this, at least,
he had the sense to reject.
But even staying home was incompatible with his nature
and he sank into depression.
Which led to his worst mistake:
Doctors he could defy, but psychiatrists
he saw as gods, and trusting them
he took their little pills
that didn't cheer him up as promised, but made him a zombie.

He was a goner, for sure,
but I should have known from his eyes,
romantic, irresistible eyes, clear
as a child's, a saint's, or a lunatic's,
that strange powers were working through him.
One day he threw away the pills
and flew off to Puerto Rico, where after a week
of sex and *animacion,* the forbidden action he thrived on,
he wrote that the cloud had lifted—
then dropped dead, just as the doctors predicted.

Walter, Walter, everyone agrees
you were a pain in the ass and a mind-fucker,
barging in in your size-thirteen shoes, interfering
with cockeyed advice, always the beachmaster,
the biggest bull walrus on the beach,
barking as you bossed us around like your harem to the end.

Your main gift to us was certainly not your poems
(even you admitted you'd need another lifetime to become a poet),
nor was it your indubitable value as an irritant
in keeping us awake,
nor even your demonstration of How to Be Old,
for one would have to be you to do as you did,
and not your will that you scrawled over,
making it practically illegible if not illegal,

but your death in action was your true estate,
a death to be studied, anthologized, included in college courses,
for your dying, your one work of art,
proved you were a master after all,
showing us how to go.

Polish Joke

(after Millen Brand)

On days when I fail at everything I try,
   I remember an ancestor on my family's Polish side,
     the one I think I take after,

who had in one of his fields a boulder,
   square in the middle,
     too large to haul away.

It was no problem really,
   but it meant no straight furrows in that field,
     and the lump of it sitting there bothered him.

According to an ancient Polish technique
   that assumes perfection possible at whatever cost,
     you dig a hole larger than the stone, right beside it,

then push it in, fill up the hole, and *voilà,*
   the rock out of sight, your field is level for plowing
     the straight furrows you demand from life. On this theory,

invented I am told by the wisest Pole who ever lived,
   my ancestor dug his hole right next to the offending boulder
     and then got down in, to begin carefully carefully

scooping out earth from under the monster stone
   to make it easier to push, so it would practically
     topple in itself, or merely with a breath—

the trick was to know
   how much of an earth support to leave
     and still have time to get out yourself.

Ninety-nine times in a hundred this worked
   and only once in a hundred failed
     when the digger took a trifle too much earth away.

This was that miserable hundredth—the stone
    that was to disappear from sight into its tomb
      and make the field flat as an ironing board

slipped from its perch too soon,
    toppling onto my earnest ancestor,
      source of my Polish genes,

and what is more, his hole
    wasn't even deep enough, so that rock still showed
      its elemental head above the ground.

Wisely making the best of it, the family
    left it there and him below
      and had the stone inscribed:

Generations to come, pay heed to folly's fate.
    He dug his grave, put himself in,
      and set the headstone over.

From Poland

"After soulless Germany," my sister writes,
"to be in an absolutely soulful land...
the zloty not buying much
even if there were anything to buy...
the bureaucracy frightening, but everyone used to it,
patiently standing on line...
sweet and helpful and unspoiled." Reading that,
I think I could live there on bread and potatoes.

Ma said that from Lamaz, her village,
Warsaw was a two-day trip by horse and wagon.
My sister writes that now "it's an hour by superhighway...

"Some old houses are still there...
a countrywoman came out of one,
her daughter in the background wearing
torn leggings and a quilted vest. We just stood
staring at each other, me in western clothes,
my passport full of border stamps.... Inside,
just a little room with a porcelain stove in the corner
and a bunk on each wall... onion skins
on the floor of boards and dirt—
cozy enough to move into at once."

Ma always said her brother, Jake, the favorite,
got to sleep on top of the stove.
She slept in the rafters with the chickens
and the barrel of herring and sack of groats to last the winter.
They called her little pig, she was so fat,
too slow for blackberrying when her sister went at dawn—
Esther yelled at her for trying to follow...
Esther, the smart one, who learned to read and write
and kept in touch with their father in America.
He was a tinsmith and when he worked on the church roof
drank with the priest. But then, he was half-goy,

the child of his mother's love affair with the landowner—
Ma told it proudly, the old scandal, but lowered her voice
to explain why she herself was always taken for Christian.
Grandma was from prosperous Jews with a farm
who never approved of the big, fair-haired tinsmith
so they eloped to poor, little Lamaz
where people lined up to read the only newspaper.

"I kept my father's photograph until we got to America,"
Ma said, "and I was happy to see him at the dock,
but when I picked up a pretty candy box in the gutter
in wonder at such a treasure being thrown away,
he smacked me across the face and called me dumbbell....
That night I tore his picture up.
I was only happy in Lamaz. Did I ever tell you,"
she tells me again, "how the milk turned sour in the pail
and we drank it that way?
There were no demands on me there," she says,
an old woman in Florida now, her children grown and gone.
"I didn't have to do anything. I could sit
eating my bowl of kasha all day long."

My sister writes: "We asked the oldest people in town
about the Jews.... None left, they told me, vaguely,
the Nazi time was the end of them, and showed me
where the Jewish cemetery had been,
a grassy area with trees, fenced in."

Generation Gap

(To the tune of "In My Life" by the Beatles)

In my high school generation
sex was made unnatural:
Simply yielding to temptation,
answering a lover's call
led more often to humiliation,
tarnishing love with guilt and pain—
and even now in times of liberation
it never will be right again.

In my pre-war generation
desire was made a laughing stock.
They sent it off to prison,
then destroyed its mind with shock,
putting mufflers on intimate sensation—
we burned with shame like a fever—
and even now in times of liberation,
love's gone wrong forever.

Tantra

While we were dancing, master,
I felt your desire unmistakably hard against me.
You weren't in the least shy about it
and reached for my prick,
but I shrank away.

Then, as if to say So okay, not that, then what?
you lay back, ready for anything,
your pale thin prick waving shamelessly in the air.

I went down on it for a moment
but your young disciples were around,
though not paying any attention—
it was just an ordinary activity to them,
their master working with a pupil.

I knew nothing sexual was the least repugnant to you,
you were willing to get on with it any way I wanted,
had guessed what I liked, and offered it,

but I was too ashamed in front of the others,
though my shame came from another time,
a different world that exists for me
more than anything in the present.

So I was the one who broke off
and lost contact.

Plea

O Noble Lord, what have I done?
From the first I was ashamed
though you did your best to serve.

Always, always, what you wanted was my pleasure
though the way you kept pushing me into danger
with several possible kinds of violence—
try to understand—
you had at all costs to be controlled.

Still, is it too late now, my dear, my stalwart gent,
to ask forgiveness, beg you to return
from your low-lying lair and wounded retirement?

Triad

A temple sculpture: Two Warriors in Combat.
Down between their knees a Female
with one of their stone pricks up her cunt,
at the same time, bending over backwards
to take the other's cock in her mouth,
while the men cross swords above her.

Even confronting each other with sharp steel,
according to this ancient mystery
something tender bridges them,
a goddess joining the warriors in her body—
for she has to be a goddess
and this is obviously her function:
But is she consoling, neutralizing,
trying to bring peace about,
or delivering the charge that sets the swords a-clashing?

Or do they only appear to fight
to deny the sexual connection below?
But no one seems to be hiding anything—
it's open as a diagram, illustrative,
rather than a daisy chain like The Three Graces.

When we say men are "joined" in battle
do we too mean like this,
opposition at one pole, concord at the other,
and in the contest both at once?
Beyond the fierce worldly display,
the glitter of rivalry, the squiring of women,
a secret brotherhood?

And this goddess created out of mutual need?
As if maleness cannot mate without a medium—
and only by a female principle can men unite . . . or fight.

Narcissus

The way I felt about myself for so long—
just another pretty face the world adored,
not in the least corresponding to the real me—
that seeing my reflection in the holy pool
I had journeyed far for and filled with my tears,
was a shocker, but frankly, what a relief
to confront the truth at last
in waters uninterested in pretty,
a depth analysis as it were.

For once feeling if not love, then tolerance,
if not approval, sympathy then,
I started treating that reflected creature better—
feeding him, caressing the high-hunched shoulders,
the tortured brow and caved-in chest,
the cold, orphaned genitals,
all so unloved-looking and neglected.
None of it had belonged to me before.

Unwanted Forever, the message in the sybilline waters:
No feeding, no caresses, will ever comfort the pain
or calm those giant fears of a child
who still needs more love than anyone can give
and who will never grow up
or learn anything more,
but, as the magic pool showed me, is mine
and mine to care for.

In the Mirror

1.

All day I look forward to that late hour
when I strip off clothes for exercises on a rug
woven, I am sure, by a jolly fat lady
who had the pattern in her mind but was divinely careless
as she chattered away with her friends at their looms.

This is my time to pay attention to important things:
In the wall mirror I gaze into my eyes
and as I move, study my body,
that map of a difficult childhood, a tortured ancestry—
it could be beautiful yet, I imagine,
and let it move as it wants to.

This is how, naked before a mirror,
I bend to the instructions in the carpet
in all possible directions, beyond the possible,
let breathing into every part of me again
until, inevitably, guided
toward caresses I didn't know I needed
I comfort myself with gentle hands.

2.

On the field of an Oriental rug,
its symbols woven so as to move in the eye,
fragments of a forgotten writing, perhaps, an old knowledge,
their convolutions, by some mysterious process,
helping me move well....

Within the elaborate borders
are rows of figures called flowers in Persian,
not one exactly like the other,
as each tree dances differently in the wind
according to the nature of its leaves.

If the woven flowers are all lopsided,
there may be a perfect one in heaven, the rug says,
but that is unattainable here.
We don't have to be perfect either,
just make stabs at it.

Don't worry, the rug seems to say as I lift my arms,
if you collect all the flowers in your eye
they'll correct each other there into a perfect one
and do the work that they are meant to—
directing your body to move as if in the garden again,
and reminding you what you forgot—
that you're a dancer.

Mae West

She comes on drenched in a perfume called Self-Satisfaction
from feather boa to silver pumps.

She does not need to be loved by you
though she'll give you credit for good taste.
Just because you say you love her
she's not throwing herself at your feet in gratitude.

Every other star reveals how worthless she feels
by crying when the hero says he loves her,
or how unhoped-for the approval is
when the audience applauds her big number—
but Mae West takes it as her due:
She knows she's good.

She expects the best for herself
and knows she's worth what she costs
and she costs plenty—
she's not giving anything away.

She enjoys her admirers, fat daddy or muscleman,
and doesn't confuse vanity and sex,
though she never turns down pleasure,
lapping it up.

Above all she enjoys her self,
swinging her body that says, Me, me, me, me,
Why not have a good time?
As long as you amuse me, go on,
I like you slobbering over my hand, big boy—
I have a right to.

Most convincing, we know all this
not by her preaching

but by her presence—it's no act.
Every word and look and movement
spells Independence:
She likes being herself.

And we who don't
can only look on, astonished.

Poems on a Theme

In Praise

The discharges of the body
are wonderful and numerous:
snot and come and spit,
the yellow stream of pee,
sweat and tears and mucus,
but best of all is shit—

let's take another look at it.

*

Who but me will celebrate
the bathroom and the running water,
the ball that floats in the toilet tank
and on older ones a pull-chain,
the hair-trap in the shower drain,
the tiles of purest porcelain,
the cabinet of fluffy towels—
and so we can be blissfully alone
with the elegant movement of our bowels,
with our assholes and our cocks—
a bathroom door that locks.

*

My shitting machine has a mind of its own:
I think of it as the sport of an off-year
like that Willys manufactured just one season
and no one bought except a schmuck
who went around lamenting he got a lemon,
parts dropping all over the road,
until far from the garage and insurance expired,
the rear-end fell out.

Testing the possibility that knowledge
might enter when the sphincter is relaxed
(don't they say bowel training in infancy
destroys the natural aptitude for learning?),
I taped on the toilet wall
a list of Japanese words and phrases,
reading them over every time
I sat down on the can,
preparing for a vacation in Japan.

The theory didn't work, though:
Not a word sank in with the outward flow—
and I didn't go.

*

It is crucial to follow the impulse
even if the bathroom is down the hall
or worse, beside the living room
as it always is when you're a guest
and everyone is out there at the table
having breakfast.

It is so easy to put off
especially when the feeling's
Can I? Should I? Dare I try?
risking a weekend of constipation
and constant farting, with difficulty silenced.
Next morning is another chance, though no guarantee,
even with lots of coffee for stimulation.

A strange house, toilet shared,
maids chatting, people rattling the knob,
anything can inhibit. Somehow the vow
must be taken to do it anyhow,
as if your mother had greeted it with joy
when you did it in your pants or on the floor

instead of in the nappy—
how she shrieked at the messy pile.
Odd that we expected her to smile....
Are we still trying not to make her unhappy?

*

Did you hear the splash?
the boy next door would ask
as I perched embarrassed on
the cold rim of the tub
and he sat on the can.

Praise Jesus, always cried
an elderly colored man
when he was done,
commemorated likewise
by religious Jews and rabbis,
regular in praise
of their Almighty One.

Shy Guy

Such a dear fellow, such a shy one,
doing his job but never praised for it,
dug at, scratched, and harshly wiped,
either ignored in public
or joked about.
Put yourself in his place:
How do you feel
when somebody calls you an asshole?

The face gets endless care and beautifying,
and though he's dying to be glamorous too,
nobody uses makeup on him.
The hair is brushed and dressed,
the hands caressed,

the eyes looked deeply into,
and even the cunt...a man I know
claims he can stare at a cunt for hours—
but who wants to gaze up an asshole?

Frustrated in his longing
for, if not public recognition,
at least appreciation, do you blame him,
ordered to squeeze himself tight
and not let out a peep for hours,
for dropping a loud one
in the middle of a cocktail party
or your big romantic moment?

We take his cooperation for granted,
and then it's all his fault, when sore with piles
or sullen in constipation,
he soon learns he gets plenty of attention,
though not the kind he craves:
We throw up our hands and submit him
to the harsh spotlight of medical procedures
or worse, the surgical amphitheatre,

never imagining what's wrong is us,
for identifying him with the shit
he so elegantly expels.

The Queen

Just looking at her, you know
she has to be a healthy shitter,
shits well and anywhere, as indeed
she would have to, with her schedule—
she can't leave the state occasion to announce
she has to go to the bathroom, or do it in her pants.

She was obviously raised by a governess
who knew what life as queen would entail
and in basics trained her sensibly,
standing for no nonsense in that department—
the resulting sphincter control
had to guide an empire, after all.

Even high and mighty, she has the look
of someone who enjoys a good crap,
that is, when she gets the chance
to sit down on the can with the daily blatt,
even if alone is out and there has to be
a lady-in-waiting alert to sound
of royal plop and splatt,
ready to pull the chain and hand over
paper roll, swan's neck, terry towels...
and congratulations.

With her as an example, the whole realm
surely on awakening moves its bowels
beautifully, in concert, as a nation.

Awards

I

The Medal of the Empire to the conductors collecting fares
on those miraculously unbattered red double-decker buses—
for running up and down the curving stairs,
calling you luv and ducky as they manipulate
levers on the machine for making change,
and cranking another gadget yoked around their necks,
spin out ticker tapes of tickets,
and all without becoming nervous wrecks.
It's not their fault it costs a fortune for a ride.

In fact, the English working class should get a prize
for putting up with the crap they take
and giving back their luv and ducky
with such kind and cheerful eyes.

They're obviously a whole other people from the lords,
those invaders from abroad who pushed them to the bottom.
Island dwellers, once safe with their surrounding sea,
they danced around the maypole thoughtlessly
until waves of conquering Teutonic hordes
herded them off to mine and mill
where they go on working for a pittance
in the legendary damp and chill,
when there are jobs at all, that is . . . O innocence . . .
It's a complete mystery to me
why they support the royals in luxury
when they could pack them off to Estoril.
But no, they dutifully offer up their asses
to the upper classes
who keep them firmly in their place.

How soulful they are, how dear,
and though it's not something they'd like to hear,
almost like an Arab race.

Awards

II

A gold medal to the inventor of the bed,
cozier than cars, less sandy than beaches.

Gold too to the genius
who invented the bathroom,
arena of the washing and fondling of the nether regions
with the ooze and stink of the forbidden,
and the miraculous flushing away.

And a medal for inventing coffee and the cigarette
that, shared, bring heads together over table tops,
making conversation intimate,
and perhaps join hands under it.
O for another lifetime to atone
for having to stop smoking in this one.

A special award for lunch, senseless but divine
eating in early afternoon,
especially things like hotdogs that are fun
to munch on walking in the sun—
I feel right now like having one!
A string of prizes certainly should
go to the brilliant inventor of food.

For clothes and its many useless pieces,
shirts with buttonholes, belts, and ties,
pleated skirts and pants with creases,
the inventor deserves a booby prize:
What a time to get them on, those complicated shapes,
instead of simple wrap-arounds and drapes.

To the inventor of romance, that world of illusion
in novel, opera, and soap opera enshrined,
another booby prize:

144

It exists only in the adolescent mind
and it's all lies.
But the biggest booby prize to the inventor
of mankind's worst tormentor, sex.
And really, let's confess, it hardly ever works.
I'm thinking not only of the sticky mess
but the urological complications, pregnancy, VD—
though I'd award a special medal for
the divinest of all inventions maybe,
sex's consolation prize, and life's, failure,
the human baby.

The Best Friend

"Hey, there's been a mistake
  in the casting end—
Ronnie's not leading man
  he's best friend."
                    —Zanuck

How's this for a movie
combining comedy and horror:
A second-rate but clever
has-been of a movie star
runs for president.
On his part it's more ambition
than criminal intent,
but men in high position
in industry and government
use him for their purposes.
At first you take it
for the joke it is,
but the plot becomes
more sinister bit by bit
as financial power under cover
of an arsenal of bombs
makes the world submit,

enslaves the human race.
The presidential twit
is a national disgrace:
How could people be so dumb
and fall for his synthetic charm,
elect a pretty face,
and, moreover, put his finger on
the button of the bomb—
the corporations' man,
the military's friend.

Though laughs it's got,
it's a grisly plot,
and believe it or not,
we're watching it all to the end.

146

Categories I: Nurses and Patients

If we divide the world into nurses and patients
I am a born nurse
and you, a born patient.

I am in a passion of taking care of you
and you demand constant, unremitting attention—
we found each other.

Your ailments increase in scope and complexity
as I struggle to keep you well,
finding cures, solutions to your problems.

Your needs are a mountain
and I am an ant
moving it grain by grain—
I daren't stop for a moment.

How to keep you alive, my darling,
when life seems to have cheated you,
rewarding you only with troubles galore.

In your view, that is somehow all my fault.
I am supposed to make it up to you,
for you see me as one of the lucky ones,
who have been given everything in life—
looks, lovers, success, and luck.

My luck, angel, is only to have found you,
the large, demanding child I adore,
the child of the world I worship,
the child of myself I care for, my sweet pain.

The more I give, the more you demand—
I can never do enough, I know. Failure, failure.
Still, I am grateful to have found

a way to be useful in life: Thank you
for that supreme gift.
To me you are a radiant being
I am honored to serve.

Nurse has found the perfect patient,
patient the perfect nurse,
and care will be unrelenting.

Both parties agree there will be no cure.

Categories II: Cows and Bulls

You can always spot a bull—
when one comes into the room
the cows flock round.

It is easy to spot two bulls—
they lock horns on sight.

It has nothing to do with gender.
Psychiatrists are wrong to encourage
every man to be the bull
and the wife the family cow
when often it's the other way—
there's no changing essences.

Raised to think they're bulls
men inside are lowing love me,
and women forced to be fluffy are born to be boss,
engendering feminist rage—okay,
bellow in protest, but if you don't
simply start being the bull you are,
sister, you're just rattling your chains.

Every couple must work out for themselves
who's bull and who's cow—
what a relief, anyhow,
not to have to play-act bull or cow,
and if you're a cow, it saves years of misery to know
not to expect from another cow
love's fireworks, though fooling around's okay
while waiting for the bull—
Don't worry, there'll be no doubt
when the real thing comes along.

As the bull said to the zebra at the zoo
     who asked him what he did,
"Take off those striped pajamas, kid,
     and I'll show you what I do."

From My Diary

A curious thing, the English word—
for plain speaking, wonderful,
but takes almost a miracle
born of adversity
or the kind of genius that I'm not
to make it sing:

Overlooking the wintry
supermarket parking lot,
tip-top on a bare tree,
a solitary bird
pouring its heart out,
breast quivering.

*

If only I was the one
before writing was discovered
to whom it occurred
that the spoken word
could be written down
or chiseled in stone,

and having only heard them spoken,
I was the one to have found
that words could each be broken
into separate units of sound,

and what was even better—
that each one of these
with elegance and ease
could be written in shape of a letter.

*

Listening to Jewish songs
reminds me of all my unshed tears.

*

Try to remember in the difficult hours:
Every problem is a teaching.

*

My instructions: Let it all go.
Let what go?
Stop asking, dummy, and just do it—
you know.

*

When he came to, people were holding his arms
trying to calm him down.

Had he actually been running around
naked through the streets, shouting
he was sick of the whole mess?

He felt terribly confused—perhaps he was insane
or at any rate out of control.

And would he go off again that way?

*

The reason I need to write poetry is
I keep forgetting important things—

like my feelings.

*

While shaving my face, I answer my critics,
marshalling rebuttals, and arguing
my right to write as I want to:
Who are you to tell me what to do? You bastards
don't have the least idea what poetry's about,
etcetera . . .

and going over and over where the chin
makes its difficult transition to the neck:
Why can't a clown for once cry real tears?

Oh, I say, waving the shaver at myself,
You pompous ass.

*

I have one eye of reality
and one of woe,
but where is my eye of pleasure?
In reality is my pleasure . . .

but I'll admit to another eye,
if you could call it an eye,
somewhere down below.

*

When I look at my face, she said,
I feel tender toward myself.

So do I,
but only when stoned.

*

I'm committed to being beautiful
but that doesn't mean I ignore
what is not its opposite but its twin—
I revel in ugliness like a new-found freedom.

*

I like only parts of waking
but every part of sleeping.

*

I still feel I should desire women
but at least I'm sure now I don't.

Stories from the Lives of My Friends (Part I)

Two, after years together, thought
an arrangement of a looser kind
might suit them better, so they split,
but in an unexpected twist of plot
one of them went blind
and they moved back in together again.
It could hardly be taken as a gift
yet, oddly, they were as happy then
as any two friends who ever lived—
though sex was not the key to it.

*

Leading him through the streets
he is like an animal beside me,
a blind lion or horse in captivity,
wind blowing through his mane,
for whom to hold on to my shoulder
is necessary, but a humiliation.

*

Guide Dog Sonnet

Some dogs live a life of ease,
playing with children, being taken out for walks,
while others, and maybe the lucky ones are these,
have to work, pulling carts, doing circus tricks,
guarding property, or as I do,
leading my master through streets to be his eyes.

There, if a friendly dog invites me to
a sniffing of assholes, an exchange of licks,
I can't forget that though I have my needs
it's in my master's safety duty lies.
And if we pass a hydrant and I've got to go
lift my leg, I must say firmly no.

Not for a biscuit do I make this sacrifice:
Being useful is how I get my kicks.

*

The Psychology of Couples

Being a couple, with the resources of two,
in public impact you benefit:
The combined effect of both of you
more than doubles it.

Being a couple is a complex game
and, brother, nothing is forgotten.
It's a lifelong struggle as you get
a death grip on each other.

As a man with much experience said:
An outsider can always tell who's on top.

*

The ears of old men
grow flaccid.
Boys' ears are crisp,
or you might say
stiff.

*

Gemini

I could easily kill
people who say
Cheer up and Smile.
But isn't it my
own cheerful streak
that overrides
my sorrow side,
refusing to take
it seriously?

154

Why shouldn't I
let myself be sad?
I believe in it,
it's the real me.
But I'm a Gemini
whose twins
do not agree:
One grins,
one's tearful,
and my sorrow side
doesn't have a chance
beside the false face
of my cheerful.

*

In the corner of the garden where I pee
the nettles grow fiercely big and bristly,
fed perhaps by something in the urine filtered through the soil,

and getting bolder, attracted by the spray
that gives their leaves a gloss,
they start leaning into the spot I aim at
so I can't fail to pee directly on them,

but undiluted, it's too hot, too strong,
and the boldest wither under it.

*

A Terrifying Line

Ladies and gentlemen,
we are approaching the German border.

*

To Whatever Future Race Survives

We seem about to destroy ourselves,
    and if we do,
I want you to know that at least
    some of us knew.

Afghanistan

Once you've been stranded in desert
you love all wetness—
the splashing of fountains at sundown in dusty plazas,
even the banal dribble of faucets,
become total pleasure.

When your ramshackle bus breaks down on a remote plain
you wait and wait, squatting in its shadow
with the robed and veiled, the more patient ones than you.
You try to take comfort from
the barren sweep of mountain ahead
and the nomad encampment visible on a far slope, as stony as this one.
The ear is assailed by a buzz of insects,
perhaps around a patch of stiff, staring-eyed sunflowers
rattled by gusts.
Something grew them there, surely,
but long ago.

No water is wet enough
to irrigate the thirst that grows here now,
though Pepsi-Cola, if there was any, would be ambrosia.
But, the ancients say,
better not drink in heat of day—wait for sundown.
Still, the imagination goes desolate,
pictures thirst-crazed lost staggerers
after illusory lakes on false horizons.

Hours, or is it days, of this,
and when you can't stand it anymore, the first change occurs,
like a shift in bedrock, a settling of the floor—
you accept being stuck there.
One place is as good as another, so why not here?
Someone begins playing a wild jangle of music
and there is even a breeze.

156

It is then that rescue comes, a truck
crowded with molten-eyed men in rakish turbans,
and you climb up onto piles of bags in back
full of some scratchy harvest of wool or wheat,
and after an hour of bumping over a stony track
the mud walls greet you of an oasis town
where intense gardens enclose pomegranate trees
at once in fruit and flower.

And finally in a caravanserai-hotel
where the men settle down cross-legged with pots of tea
on rug-draped divans in the gloom
comes the ultimate, soul-drenching blessing in the desert world,
the world of the ancestors, of the old power:

In your room you strip off dust-caked clothes
down to tender skin, pores open to everything now,
and turn on the shower.

To Love

Away from home on a tour in the West
I worried about you constantly, my dearest,
until I had a dream one night where you
were a large plant I was chopping down with a shovel:
First I slashed off your feet
and then battered your head in, that head
that has already been attacked
by scalpel, drill, and saw,
and is always blindly bumping things,
making my heart ache.

I woke in a sweat of course
but after the shock wore away that I
could do such a thing to you, my angel, even in a dream,
I saw how absolutely necessary it was—
your needs had pursued me across a continent
and this was the only way of getting free, of renouncing
even for a week the relentless care of you,
the concern of my days and nights: How to keep you,
an exotic, delicate plant, alive in an arctic clime—
though in my dream, I must admit,
you were a vigorous weed, overtopping me.

And then, my leafy, my green one,
whom I water daily and put in the sun,
after chopping you down and shoveling you away
I could leave you in God's hands—
and loving you not the less for being free,
went almost light-hearted on with my journey.

To Poetry

(to the tune of "An Die Musik" by Schubert)

How often have I fled your gentle bondage
to seek beyond the boundaries of art,
You offered more than a discipline of language
but still I longed for another kind of voyage—
through nocturnal ways of the heart.

Impassioned to discover what life was concealing,
I hardly turned to you until despair
had flung me down—I was drowning in my feelings—
when unsought words came like tears, a gift of healing,
and like a rescuer you were there.

Whatever time is left to offer homage,
there's one important thing I have learned:
No better way than accept your gentle bondage—
my least effort devoted to your service
has been a thousand fold returned.

About the Author

Edward Field has received the Lamont Award from the Academy of American Poets, the Shelley Prize from the Poetry Society of America, a Guggenheim Fellowship, and the Prix de Rome from the National Academy. He has published several popular novels pseudonomously. Edward Field lives in New York City.

Books by Edward Field

Stand Up, Friend, With Me, Grove Press (1963)
Variety Photoplays, Grove Press (1967)
Eskimo Songs and Stories, Delacorte Press (1973)
Sweet Gwendolyn and the Countess, Konglomerati Press (1976)
A Full Heart, Sheep Meadow Press (1977)
Stars in My Eyes, Sheep Meadow Press (1978)